The Green Historical Walking

CW00673966

Mark Alexander .

This book is dedicated to The Friends of Littlemoor Park (Queensbury) in recognition of their part in the fight against Bradford Council in the attempt to site a crematorium in this most precious place.

All the walks contained within this Historical Walking guide can be completed using only public transport therefore making it "Green" and ethical.

The Stags Head Publishing Company (Queensbury)

ISBN: 9798617946354

Contents

North Baildon to Menston Village

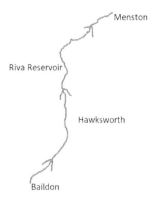

This walk commences by the strangely named Potted Meat Stick in the centre of the old village of Baildon. The village is reached from Bradford Interchange by buses 662,622,676,634. The approximate distance of this walk is 5.5 miles

The Potted Meat Stick, or to give it the correct name of The Ferrand Memorial Fountain was first placed in the centre of Baildon in 1862. According to contemporary news reports, the monument stood in the middle of Baildon for about a century but the road needed reorganisation and development and at that time, the local Council thought that it would cost about £150 to destroy the monument but £400 to move it.

Eventually, it was agreed that the fountain would be removed and replaced as soon as funds would permit. Alas, this never happened and about twenty years later it was found damaged and in pieces on wasteland on the other side of Bradford. The Bradford Council paid to have the monument re-erected in October 1986, not far from the original site. The nickname of "Potted Meat Stick" is believed to come from the colour of the pink granite part of the column.

From here you move off in the direction of the moors that began on the north edge of the village. Walking past the streetside rows of former mill workers cottages, you take the foot gate at the side of the deep cattle grid just up the road.

The noise that the traffic makes as it passes over the grid must surely annoy the nearby householders as it is an almost constant thud thud thud. From here the moors will not end until you pass over Hawksworth Moor and drop down towards Menston village. Staying on the main road you take the footpath through the bracken that lines the side of Hawksworth Road on the right and skirt along the side of the disused Low Eaves Delph.

Baildon Moor is an ancient place with a long and important history of pre-Industrial Revolution quarrying and coal mining. The stone that was heaved from the ground across the moors was used in many of the local buildings and even some further afield. The coal was used to heat the humble cottages in the village and later on to create steam to power the local mills. The simple path takes you past an old cottage named Whitehouse on the edge of the moor. The whitewashed building was built in 1730 and was used as a tea room for the moor walkers at one point in the past.

Now your path takes you closer to the main road as you approach the tiny hamlet of Low Hill with its magnificent former Methodist Chapel on the left. Originally thirteen cottages stood here but today only four remain plus the Chapel which is also now a private residence.

The maximum population of Low Hill was 96 in 1861, but was reduced to 26 by the 1891 census. The cottages were built by the Lord of the Manor Abraham Maud of Rylstone near Skipton. They were built to house miners who worked the small coal pits across the moor and most of them were demolished in the slum clearances in the 1960s. The remaining cottages only received mains electricity in 1980.

The Methodist chapel cost £500 to build in 1874 and people from Low Hill, Moorside, Low Springs and Sconce would worship here. In its heyday, it held very popular fundraising concerts and was noted for the large attendances at open-air services. As the population fell, so did attendances, until the congregation was less than ten. The chapel closed in 1917 and was sold for £320, becoming a tea room for some time in the 1930s.

From here you continue along the roadside footpath towards another tiny hamlet named Low Springs. This is officially part of Hawksworth and therefore also part of the Leeds district. One has to be careful now as the path has ended and you have to walk on the road.

The traffic speeds by at an alarming speed considering the narrowness of the road as you pass by the end of Sconce Lane before following the winding country road uphill towards Potter Brow Bridge. Glancing up and looking over your right shoulder you can see Idle Hill rising majestically in the distance. It appears to be so far away even though it is not, and it is visible from just about everywhere from over the Bradford district.

From here the road winds around between Honey Joan Wood and Honey Joan Hill and before long you are alongside the site of the former Hawksworth Mill. This substantial 15th-century former corn mill stood on the left side of the road and was served by water from nearby Jum Beck. The water stored in the millpond powered the mill's waterwheel which in turn provided motive power to its basic machinery. This beck still runs into Gill Beck in the valley between Hawksworth and Baildon and then runs into the River Aire. The mill was burned down by Luddites coming back from breaking frames in Guiseley.

From this point you carry on for a short distance and after passing Intake Farm arrive at Four Lane Ends. This is the area where Mill lane, Goose Lane, Old lane and Hillings Lane all meet. Now straight ahead to climb Hillings Lane then you turn right along Odda Lane. This takes you past the 150-year-old Sandstone quarry named Odda Delph towards a demolished Wesleyan Methodist Chapel. Built in 1837 on land leased for one hundred years from Francis Hawksworth Fawkes, this Chapel was torn down in 1902 when a new one was constructed further down. The site was used to extend the graveyard which can still be seen along the side of the road.

This new Chapel built in 1903 at a cost of £940 had seating for 120 people. Designed by the Bradford firm of Walker and Collinson, the opening service was conducted outside due to the large number of people present. At the junction of Main Street and Old Lane, you turn along Old Lane and pass by the former village Pinfold and head towards Goose Lane and Jum Bridge. All along this road the drystone walls are low and the fields with their grazing cattle and sheep just seem to open up all the way back to the high moorland of Baildon.

In the distance, the bracken and heather covered land sweeps upwards till it reaches the summit of Baildon Moor. Between here and there the pastoral fields seem to roll on forever. The road you are now travelling along was once a continuation of Old lane but has subsequently been renamed as Goose Lane.

You still have to take great care on the narrow country lane as you approach Reva Reservoir. Constructed in an area known as Whin Hills and completed in 1874, this 1.2-kilometre long body of water is home to a sailing and canoe centre as well as providing water for the city of Bradford a few miles in the distance. Many varieties of birdlife can be seen here and it is, in fact, a popular spot for the areas Ornithologists.

At the end of Goose Lane you cross over Bingley Road at Intake Gate to start the trek over Hawksworth Moor towards the village of Menston. Here there is an area marked on the old Ordnance Survey maps as an area of "Quick Sands". This runs alongside the beaten footpath you are now on.

Here you will notice what is known as a Catchwater. This is a concrete-lined ditch complete with associated pipes and a sluice gate at the end. Its purpose is to literally catch the water as it runs off the moor from its numerous small streams around the area of Black Beck and White Flush.

At this point the moorland is flat and expansive with only dry stone walls to break the land. Away to your right, Reva Hill rises up as if to stand guard over the nothingness that surrounds you. At 900 metres above sea level, it must have been a valued place for the pre-historic humans who once roamed the area. On the far horizon the communications intercept and missile warning site of RAF Menwith Hill is just visible. Between the horizon and Reva Hill can be seen mighty Otley Chevin.

This whole area is littered with Limestone Boulder pits, tiny Delphs and age-old marker stones. Centuries ago it would have been a hive of human activity but now is inhabited only by walkers, pheasants and the men who shoot them. Here you turn off to the right and started to make your way over Stocks Hill and down towards Menston.

After perhaps twenty minutes brisk walking you reach the former Hawksworth Moor Service Reservoir on Hillings Lane. This had laid derelict since the Yorkshire Water restructuring exercises of 1995 but has recently been refurbished to contain a smart house. Excavation of the site began in May 1903 and the construction was completed in August 1904. The roof has now been torn off but the surrounding stone walls are still in great condition considering they had been underwater for decades.

To the left of this area you drop down from the high wall into a small gulley where you will find Dry Beck. This beck forms the ancient boundary between Menston and Burley Woodhead. From here it is only a few yards to Moor Road where you can make your way towards the hamlet of Burley Woodhead and the wooded remains of a former Bleachworks.

From this point you pass by centuries old weatherbeaten quarry workers cottages. Situated right on the roadside their presence affords no respite as there are no bushes to sink into to let the cars past. Eventually you reach a small track on the right that leads you down towards a tiny collection of cottages. These were once the homes of the workers at Rombalds Moor Bleachworks Mill. Built in the 1850s and once owned by Joseph Gill, this mill was operational until 1927.

The workers would bleach the yarns from local Linen mills in a collection of buildings surrounding a series of mill ponds. By 1918, the manufacture of Linen yarn had declined and Gill and Son turned to the treatment of Cotton rag. The 1871 census shows James McKinley as the manager, and by 1900, it employed forty people. It was closed after local landowners protested about pollution in the local waterways. The millponds silted up and nature returned. Today only the former mill cottage survives.

Upon reaching the end of the settlement of cottages, you enter a field through a stone stile. Here you can see a stone chimney standing proudly in the wood only a few feet away. To the side are the remains of a wall and a weir that ran along the beck. The site is covered by decades of plant growth but the remains are still clearly visible.

At this point the trees are sparse but the vegetation is not and it can sap the strength as you wade through it towards the open fields that lay beyond. From here the occasional train can be heard as it runs along the distant line towards Menston Station.

After crossing the fields you climb the fence onto Clarence Drive. This sleepy country lane is lined by massive detached houses owned no doubt by people of some wealth. In the space of a few minutes, you will be sitting at Menston railway station waiting for the next Bradford bound train.

Haworth Circle (including Worth Valley Railway)

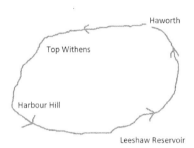

Keighley is reached from Bradford Interchange by the 662 bus. Alternatively you can begin the walk in Haworth after taking a short trip on the Worth Valley railway. The approximate distance of this walk is 5.5 miles.

This walk involves something a little different if one wishes to go down that route. The notion of a trip on the wonderful Worth Valley Railway meets with most peoples approval and merge with some Bronte history, a bit of walking and fresh air and you have a memorable walk.

This journey starts at splendid Keighley Railway Station. Here the station platform is resplendent in its ornate roof girders and supports, all decked in the company colours of cream and burgundy which conveys something of a 1940s feeling.

The Keighley and Worth Valley Railway is a 5-mile-long branch line that runs from Keightley and Oxenhope which once served mills and villages in the Worth Valley and is now a heritage railway line. It connects to the national rail network at Keighley Railway Station. The railway was incorporated by an Act of Parliament in 1862 and the first sod was cut on Shrove Tuesday, 9 February 1864 by Isaac Holden, the chairman of the Keighley and Worth Valley Railway.

The railway was originally constructed as a single-track line, but with a trackbed wide enough to allow upgrading to double-track if the need arose in the future. The rails were completed in 1866, track laying having started at each end before being joined in the middle. The line was tested with a locomotive from Ilkley, which took nearly two hours to get from Keighley to Oxenhope, but just thirteen minutes to get back. The opening ceremony was held on Saturday 13 April 1867 and in 1962 British Railways closed the line in 1962 with their last scheduled passenger train running on 31 December 1961.

A preservation society was formed which bought the line from British Rail and reopened it in 1968 as a heritage railway. The line is now a major tourist attraction operated by 500+ volunteers and roughly ten paid staff, and it carries more than 110,000 passengers a year. The railway is currently one of only two preserved railways which operate a complete branch line in its original form. The line and its stations have been used in numerous period film and television productions including the film The Railway Children and the BBC comedy Last of the Summer Wine.

After only a few minutes the train comes to a halt at Ingrow West Station. Like Keighley and the other stations on the line, this is a traditional station with a tiny waiting room and ticket office. From here, the next stop on this nostalgia trip is Damens station, the smallest standard-gauge railway station in Britain, and still lit by gas lamps

The next stop is the station at Oakworth. Restored to Edwardian condition, this station is also lit by gas lamps. From here it only takes a few minutes before you arrive in the historic village of Haworth. The station at Haworth is on the outskirts of the village and from there it is quite a hike up Main Street. The village of Haworth is a major tourist attraction due to its links with the Bronte family and the Worth Valley Railway, and tourism accounts for much of the local economy.

The cobbles of Main Street wind up past Bed and Breakfast houses, bookshops, cafes and even the odd pub. The Black Bull is probably the most famous as it was here that Branwell Bronte was reputed to have begun his decline into alcoholism and opium addiction. The street is narrow and lined with rows of 17th-century cottages all displaying beautiful hanging baskets of flowers and immaculately scrubbed stone front steps.

Here, the people are proud and they have to be to keep the hordes of visiting tourists happy and spending money. And why not as it is a beautiful and historic place and they should rightly be proud of living there.

Main Street turns into Bronte Street but the quaint old cottages just keep on coming. Eventually you will arrive at the junction with West Street. This is opposite a small Baptist Chapel and its graveyard. Stop here for a few minutes to admire the aged graves.

From here you leave Haworth along West Street, passing by more rows of immaculately kept terraced cottages, with the fields opposite bearing the scars of past quarrying. The road continues on towards Stanbury but you take a left turn along Cemetery road towards the moors. Glancing over to your left, the rising heights of Penistone Hill with its massive quarries on the other side can clearly be seen.

Only a short distance along Cemetery Road is the old Haworth Cemetery. Consecrated in 1893 this cemetery contains the grave of Lily Cove, an intrepid but unfortunate female Balloonist. She died aged 21 when her parachute failed to open whilst demonstrating a quick descent from a balloon over the Worth Valley at the Haworth Gala in 1906.

Standing here on the road opposite the cemetery gates, you can admire the view across the valley, over the river Worth and across to Pickles Hill. The patchwork of fields on the far valley side could be full of Sheep and their lambs basking in the early afternoon warmth but this is dependant on the time of year. It is the kind of scene that you see printed on biscuit tins the world over.

At this point the magnificent Lower Laithe Reservoir can be seen standing proudly in the valley bottom. Opened in 1925 by The Marquis of Hartington and constructed by stone heaved from the ground at nearby Dimple Quarry, this reservoir holds a huge and impressive body of water. The thick clay that lines it was transported by narrow gauge railway from its source near Top Withens.

The small farm of Lower Laithe was submerged during the reservoir's construction and lies somewhere deep beneath the 60 feet of water to this day. Construction of the dam had actually begun before World War I but was interrupted and only completed in 1925.

Continuing along this lane you soon pass the narrow moorland track which skirts past the 17th-century farmhouse of Hill Top with its imposing views of the nearby reservoir. Bleak moorland stretches away to your left giving a foretaste of the terrain which will come in abundance in a short while. After a short walk you reach the crossroads with Moorside Road. Here the landscape is dotted with small delphs where much of the stone on which Haworth is built was quarried from the ground by hardworking local men.

Passing by the wonderfully isolated Springs Farm, you will found that the track rises up gradually as it winds its way along the side of the valley. It is here in the area known as Jos Hill that the valley narrows in and takes on a steeper appearance. Along the valley floor runs South Dean Beck and it is here that the famed Bronte waterfall can be found. The picturesque but unspectacular waterfall on the moors above Haworth is fed by Lumb Beck which then joins South Dean Beck. Further on back towards Haworth it then feeds into Laithe Reservoir.

The gentle burbling of the beck as it runs under the ancient clapper bridge gives this small area something of a mystical feeling. From this point you head for the long-abandoned farmstead of Top Withens, on which it is said Emily Bronte based her ruins of Wuthering Heights. That fact is disputed as she never actually came here.

The ruins of Top Withens certainly are remote and windswept even on a fine day. What the area would be like in the depths of a bleak mid-winter can only be guessed at. But from here the view across the moors is superb and unrivalled with the wind turbines on the moors above Denholme clearly visible. From here you take a small rocky path that leads in the direction of the moor top.

The path is uneven and slows your progress but after perhaps thirty minutes you should reach the summit of the moor and turn off in the direction of Haworth onto another tiny path which follows the line of a deep drainage ditch cut in the soil.

There is nothing but the occasional stone marker post in this bleak wilderness. Unlike Rombalds Moor, there were no ruins, cairns or drystone walls to break the scenery. From here you must begin to descend from Harbour Hill towards Spa Hill. Here the vast open moorland begins to change to banks of thick heather and you must follow the high wire perimeter fence of a plantation. Here the heather almost blocks out the available light it is that tall. The stems are long, thick and tough, with the soil threatening to turn your ankles at any time.

From here you must follow what appears to be part of a conduit. Follow this for a while and it is only a short climb up the far side of the gully which leads to Leeshaw Reservoir. Once past the reservoir, the tiny hamlet of Marsh is only a mile away and from there it is only a short walk back into Howarth. From here you can catch either the bus or the Worth Valley train back to Keighley and beyond.

Blackstone Edge Moor to Todmorden Via Stoodley Pike

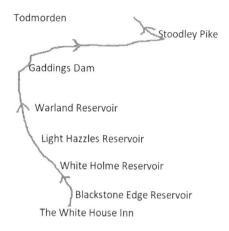

Todmorden

Stoodley Pike

Gaddings Dam

Warland Reservoir

Light Hazzles Reservoir

White Holme Reservoir

Blackstone Edge Reservoir

The White House Inn

Blackstone Edge Moor is reached by buses X58 or 590 from Halifax. The approximate distance of this walk is 6.0 miles.

The small bus from Halifax will drop you directly outside the White House public house but it is not a designated stop so you must inform the driver of your intention beforehand. This isolated pub was formerly known as The Coach and Horses and that title gives an indication of its former use on the important historical transport route from Halifax to Littleborough and Rochdale.

From here the route is flat and level until you reach Stoodley Pike on the far side of the moor then the topography drops sharply down towards Todmorden and Hebden Bridge. You are walking upon the top of the Pennines, the roof of England in fact.

Blackstone Edge is a gritstone escarpment which rises to 1,549 feet above sea level in the Pennine hills on the boundary between Greater Manchester and West Yorkshire. Passing over the crag is Blackstone Edge Long Causeway, also known as Blackstone Edge Roman Road, a paved road originally thought to be of Roman origin. After investigations by James Maxim it is now considered to be a 1735 turnpike or packhorse route.

The Aiggin Stone, a gritstone pillar or possibly a way-marker, stands alongside the packhorse route and marks the county boundary. The stone has a cross and the letters I and T cut into it. Its name is said to derive from the French aiguille for a needle or aigle for an eagle.

Much of the surrounding area was within the ancient parish of Huddersfield, although some parts lay within Butterworth township. In the English Civil War the Parliamentarians sent 800 men to fortify Blackstone Edge; John Rosworm came from Manchester to direct the construction of defences. It was successfully held against an attack by Royalist cavalry.

In 1846 a meeting of supporters of Chartism from the surrounding industrial towns of Lancashire and Yorkshire was held on the moor, attracting up to 30,000 people.

This walk takes you past five reservoirs which were constructed by The Rochdale Canal Company to service their canal down in the valley on the far side of the moor. During the First World War, the government took control of the canals, and when they were handed back in August 1920, the Rochdale canal was in financial trouble.

In 1923, the Oldham and Rochdale Corporations Water Act paved the way for the transfer of its eight reservoirs, Blackstone Edge, Easterly Gaddings Dam, Higher and Lower Chelburn, Hollingworth Lake, Light Hazzles, Warland and Whiteholme reservoirs, to those corporations to supply drinking water.

The first one you come to is Blackstone Edge reservoir which is upon you almost immediately after you pass the access gate to the moor. The path skirts alongside the western edge of the reservoir following the line of a regulating drain.

The exceptionally fine views start from here as Manchester, Rochdale and Oldham can now be seen far away in the distance. At this height the weather can change in an instant and you should always be aware of this.

As you walk along the track, ancient and strange rock formations rise on your right at Cow Head. Here Chelburn Moor stretches away to your left but you have to press on and continue the journey towards Utley Edge. Look out for the tiny packhorse like footbridge across the drain at this point to your right. Passing Light Hazzles Edge on your right you come to a sizable sluice at the very end of Light Hazzles reservoir. This reservoir is connected to the much larger White Holme Reservoir which can be seen away to your right as you pass by.

The track continues on a level plane through the lunar-like landscape as you approach the largest of the reservoirs that you will encounter. Warland Reservoir is as you would expect, full and functional for most of the time but on one occasion recently it was drained for restorative work. With the reservoir being empty the brooding wreck of a barge was visible.

A barge at this height on the moors seems such a bizarre sight but not so when you understand the reason why. Apparently, during WW2, three such barges were driven by road then launched into the water before being chained together in a line across the reservoir. The reason for this was to deter any attempted landing by german airborne forces in the event of an invasion. No invasion came so the barges were scuttled sometime after the end of hostilities.

From here the track follows the line of the huge embankment and you follow this towards Warland drain which lies at the far end. After three hundred yards or so the drain doglegs to the right and it is here that you turn left along a footpath and head towards Langfield Common and Gaddings Dam.

Gaddings Dam West lies in the heart of Langfield Common, an area of moorland above Lumbutts and Mankinholes in the Upper Calder Valley. Originally constructed as two dams (East and West), the eastern-most dam, which is now empty and has been permanently breached by its owners, United Utilities, was the earlier of the two dams. This was built by the Rochdale Canal Company in the early 1800s to supply water to the canal in the valley below.

Water was captured for both Gaddings Dams (East and West) from distant streams through the Gaddings Drain. The remains of a complex of sluice gates and waterways can still be traced on the moorland around the dams. The drain itself had nine stone bridges to allow livestock to pass freely.

The dam is reputed to have been built using convict labour from Manchester and has something of a less than glorious past. On May 2, 1872, William Proctor, of Brook Street, Todmorden, who had been missing for some time, was found drowned in the dam.

At 3.45 in the morning of July 20, 1889, the bodies of three boys were recovered from the dam, having drowned whilst bathing. They were James Stevenson (12 years old), Abraham Crossley (10 years old) and Ernest Greenwood (9 years old). All were from nearby Hollins.

On March 17, 1894, at about 11.00 am, the body of Edward Ogden, 57 years old, of Queen Street, Cobden, Todmorden, was removed from Gaddings. He had been missing for some days.

On April 20, 1890, Gaddings Dam was used as a venue for a prizefight between two men from Whitworth. Thirty-six rounds were fought, with both combatants taking a bruising. Today it imparts more of a peaceable feeling and is host to the second bizarre sight on this walk; a beach some 1200 feet above sea level above Todmorden in West Yorkshire.

The beach itself is somewhat tiny and sits in one corner of the dam. It consists of sandstone particles that are the result of eons of wind erosion of the surrounding sandstone rocks. Depending on the time of year of your visit it may be crammed full of families enjoying their day out at Englands highest beach.

Upon leaving Gaddings Dam you head towards the monument of Stoodley Pike. To do this you have to cross Langfield Common by way of a well-defined footpath which passes over Black Clough, Spittle Clough and Heeley Clough, a distance of 1.8 miles in total.

Stoodley Pike is a 1,300-foot hill and is noted for the 121-foot Stoodley Pike Monument which stands on the summit. The monument dominates the moors of the upper Calder Valley and the market towns of Todmorden and Hebden Bridge below.

The monument is near the villages of Mankinholes and Lumbutts, and was designed in 1854 by local architect James Green. It was completed in 1856 at the end of the Crimean War.

The monument replaced an earlier structure, which was started in 1814 and commemorating the defeat of Napoleon and the surrender of Paris. It was completed in 1815, after the Battle of Waterloo (Napoleonic Wars), but collapsed in 1854 after an earlier lightning strike and decades of weathering. Its replacement was therefore built slightly further from the edge of the hill. During repair work in 1889 a lightning conductor was added, and although the tower has since been struck by lightning on numerous occasions, no notable structural damage is evident.

There is evidence to suggest that some sort of structure existed on the site even before the earlier structure was built. The monument is approximately two miles south-west of Hebden Bridge and approximately 2.5 miles east of Todmorden town centre. The monument was Grade II listed in 1984.

Upon leaving Stoodley Pike you take another well-defined footpath which descends down the hillside directly in front of the monument. This leads you onto a track named Moorland View which runs alongside the site of the long-gone Fielden Hospital for Infectious Diseases on your right. Turn left at the junction with Lee Bottom Road and walk for approximately five hundred yards until you reach Broad Gate. Here you turn right and continue along the track through the woods before crossing the canal. From here it is only a short distance to the main Halifax road where you can catch the bus from Todmorden to return to Halifax and thus complete your journey.

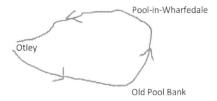

Otley is reached by taking the 653 bus from Bradford Interchange, and the approximate distance for this walk is six miles.

The market town of Otley is a sizable town and until recently was reputed to possess more public houses per head of population than any other town in England. This walk can be commenced from any point in the town centre and if you have arrived by bus, the station is central and provides a convenient start off point. You begin this walk by leaving the town centre via Leeds Road. This road is an ancient route between Otley and the top of Pool Bank and ultimately leads to Bramhope beyond that.

Moving past the splendid Junction Inn on the left, you walk along Gay Lane and soon reach the end of Albion Street. Here you have to open your stride somewhat to accommodate the rising incline of Leeds Road as you head towards Pool Bank. The small roundabout connecting Leeds Road with the Otley bypass is reached in no time.

This is the spot where the Otley branch of the Ilkley and Otley railway line passed underneath via a tunnel. Today the route of the former train line can be walked as it carries on down through some woods and on towards Pool-in-Wharfedale. The line in the other direction ran to Otley Station but today the former trackbed carries part of the Otley bypass and is best avoided at all costs due to the fast-flowing traffic.

The imposing Gothic Victorian house named Brunswick Villa looms into view on the left a little further on. Set back slightly from the road and fronted by short but stout railings the house imparts an image of Victorian splendour and of an age gone by. Today it is probably the family home to a cocksure city slicker who makes his pile in Leeds, but back in its heyday, it will have belonged to a Victorian of some standing and position.

The road continues to rise up towards Pool Bank, flanked by rolling meadows dropping down the valley on one side, and the ancient and brooding Danefield Woods on the right. This dark and rather depressing plantation creates something of a foreboding feeling over the stretch of road that lies ahead. Just before the point where the road kinks to the right as it passes over the tiny beck named Holbeck Scar, you arrive at the site of a ghastly daytime murder of an Otley Mother and Housewife.

On Tuesday 5th May 1908 it had been raining incessantly and the road surface was but a sea of muddy ruts caused by the passing horse-drawn and occasional engine driven traffic. Mother of three Elizabeth Todd, aged 31, was stabbed to death at the roadside by a 21-year-old tearaway from the North-East named James Jefferson. She was thrown over the wall into the field to the left of where you now stand and decapitated for good measure. Jefferson had been hacking feverishly at her pale white neck with a filleting knife, and within seconds, he had managed to completely sever her head and fling it twenty feet into the field. His short-cropped blond hair was streaked with the blood that was still pumping from the headless torso that he held in front of him.

He then proceeded to attempt to cut off one of her arms. Sawing with his knife like the mad man that he obviously was, he appeared to be completely oblivious to the presence of the two burly men who were grappling with him. Eventually Jefferson was pulled from the corpse and hauled off to Otley to await his fate.

Mrs Todd had lived with her family in an old quarry worker's cottage a short distance further along Leeds Road, and this simple abode you will pass in a few minutes. Today only a small length of the roadside wall remains to pay respect to the memory of this tragic murder.

When your lust for blood and gore is satisfied, you may continue along Leeds Road pass by the reputedly haunted Little Stubbing Farm as it comes into view on the left-hand side. Haunted by a restless past occupant, this building is avoided at all costs by the locals according to some. Glance down to your left and you can see Caley Hall, glance to your right and the spectre of Caley Crags with Caley Deer Park beyond come into view.

A couple of hundred yards further on you will notice a rusty old set of iron gates that once led to the long-gone house named Glen Royd. Built in 1880 this house was occupied in 1909 by Frank Whitaker, a member of the quarry owning family at Pool Bank. It was demolished around 1960 apparently due to subsidence and today no trace remains.

A little further along on the left you now approach the row of cottages named Crag View (or Quarry View) where Elizabeth Todd and her family lived. Constructed in 1880 by Benjamin Whitaker & Sons, this stout row of cottages originally housed some of the workers from their nearby quarry. It was from one of the central cottages that Elizabeth Todd left at 4 pm to make the daily six miles round trip to visit her Mother in Otley. Of course, she never arrived and her final trip was in a horse-drawn hearse to the cemetery on Pool Road.

Pool Bank Quarry was split into two areas, with both the nearby quarry and the one further down Old Pool Bank Road ultimately being owned by the Whitaker family. In 1846, the lower quarry was listed as being owned by James Bray. It was Bray who donated the magnificent tombstone in the image of one of the castellated portals of Bramhope tunnel which stands in the graveyard at Otley Parish Church.

This is dedicated to the memory of the twenty-three men who died during the construction of nearby Bramhope Tunnel. It was during his tenure that the quarry produced stone to build the nearby Arthington Viaduct as well as the interior of the tunnel. Leeds Town Hall, Otley Civic Centre, and the reservoirs further up Wharfedale at Fewston and Swinsty also benefited from the stone heaved out of the ground on Pool Bank.

Right across the road from Crag View (Quarry View) is Quarry Road, the main service road off Leeds Road. On the left was the Quarry Masters house whilst opposite were three cottages (now as one). Groves Terrace, originally wooden bungalows, was demolished in 1939 and rebuilt as seen today. It was in this area where a 22 chamber brick kiln was being operated by Whitakers around 1900. They made use of the clay and a sandy substance which had previously been removed to access the quarry stone.

The resulting bricks were not considered to be of a very high standard but could be used for underground work and out of sight walls. The price was eighteen shillings per thousand at the quarry, two shillings extra if taken to the railway station.

Pool Bank Quarry eventually closed in 1915 but re-opened in 1920, remaining in operation until 1939. After the closure of the upper quarry and brickworks, the area was used in various ways during WW2. Broken bricks from the brickworks, which had been disposed of in a pit, were removed and used as hardcore for the base of the Avro factory that was being built at Yeadon.

The sides of the quarry were some three hundred feet high and Canadian soldiers from Farnley Camp near Otley trained here. They used the quarry face for climbing, abseiling and also hand grenade practice.

The quarries were worked by horses until 1895 when a steam Locomotive was purchased to work in the top quarry. The quarry was just under a mile from the railway station and some 300 feet above the railway line. From the quarry to the station the incline was 650 yards. This incline was negotiated by using gravity; allowing loaded wagons, or bogies, on their way down to pull empty bogies up. The operation was controlled by a cable brake drum north of Far Row cottages.

In these early days, before a bridge was built over the main road it was crossed by the bogey line but at such an angle that a turntable was needed. This was situated to the north of the road near the old Toll Bar House. This was the same building that you can now see ahead.

The tramline crossed over Leeds Road by way of a metal bridge. The abutments can still be seen and the one right on the bend in the road seems to attract motorcyclists to smash into it when they fail to take the tight right-hand bend. There have been more than a few deaths at this spot.

In May 1941, the road was closed for four hours whilst the bridge, known as "the slide", was dismantled for scrap. This was used to help in the Second World War effort. It is thought that some of the melted down metal was used in the construction of Lancaster bombers at the nearby Avro factory at Yeadon.

As you reach the old Toll Bar house, the road forks left along Pool Bank Old Road, and as you walk along here it is easy to understand why the field to the left is marked on the old maps as Horse Pasture Plantation. It was the perfect place to rest the horses that worked the quarry prior to the steam engine arriving.

What a veritable hive of activity this now peaceful little area would have been in the past. The incessant tapping of hammers will have reverberated around the slopes of the Wharfedale valley and be heard for miles around. No explosives were ever used at Pool Bank quarries as this caused fissures in the stone and it all had to be worked by hand.

Pool Bank Old Road has quite an incline as it drops down towards the site of the long-gone Pool Railway Station. On the right at the top you will notice Bar House Row, which stands proudly like a sentinel overlooking the valley that stretches out before it.

Built in 1879 using stone from Fairy Dell at the bottom part of Old Pool Bank Quarry, this majestic row of houses enjoys fantastic views across the Wharfedale and Washburn valleys. You can even make out Almscliffe Crag some four miles away in the distance if the day is clear.

For such a narrow lane, Pool Bank Old road is surprisingly busy with traffic. No doubt due to travellers making use of it to avoid the longer trip via the new Pool Bank New Road. You are now headed towards the village of Pool-in-Wharfedale down below. Carry on down the hill and soon you will pass by another picturesque row of cottages named Sandy Lobby.

Constructed in 1887, the end cottage overlooking the valley housed the quarry foreman and the other cottages housed the workers. The deeds of some cottages on Sandy Lobby state that the road should only be used for quarry traffic. As late as 1950 there was a gate leading up above into the quarry from here.

After only a few minutes walking you arrive at the bottom of the hill and the area where Pool-in-Wharfedale Railway Station used to lie. Willow Court now stands here in its place. The station was opened in 1865 and closed exactly a century later as part of the Beeching cuts in 1965.

This station was a hive of activity during the Second World War. New tanks and stores arrived from the Leeds armament factories to be stored at Riffa Camp and Farnley Military Camp. A special ramp was built on the platform for ease of loading and these movements were usually made during the night. An accident occurred one night in 1941, killing Joseph Bateson, a Leeds tannery owner whilst he was returning home to Fairlea (now White Croft) on Arthington Lane. His chauffeur-driven Rolls Royce was in collision with a tank which was without lights because of wartime blackout restrictions. It had turned into the station when the car ran into the rear of the tank.

Otley Bridge was not considered strong enough to take this heavy traffic so Pool Bridge and Pool Station were used. When a particularly heavy piece of equipment was moved to the Camps it was unloaded at Arthington Station and driven across the river at Arthington's ancient Castley Ford. At one time a large movement of tanks rumbled through the village which was thought to be en-route for the Normandy Landing.

About a week prior to all this activity the base camp at Farnley was at different times visited by King George, Winston Churchill, and Viscount Bernard Montgomery. Today no trace of Pool-in-Wharfedale Railway station remains and the only evidence of the area's former use is a stone bridge that carries the road over the former trackbed.

Arriving at the junction with Pool Bank New Road, you start to skirt along the great outer wall of Old Pool Hall. This extensive six-bedroom Grade II Listed Manor House blends a modern interior with character features. This property is accessed via a lovely private driveway and enjoys a cobbled parking forecourt to the front and an enclosed rear garden complete with a Victorian Gazebo. Ornate tall fireplace's, exposed beams, mullioned arched windows, and 17th-century history right where you would never expect it.

With old pool Hall behind you, you make your way through the village towards the river Wharfe and the turn off for Otley. Along the main road and on your right you will notice bricked up old doorways aplenty in the row of stone cottages next to The Half Moon pub. Quaint St Wilfrids church complete with village war memorial in front stands across the road. Further along, more rows of sandstone cottages line the right-hand side of the road, whilst opposite stands Pool Methodist Church.

After walking only a few hundred yards along Pool Road towards Otley, you will notice a small stone bus shelter on your left. You may have noticed one exactly the same between Elizabeth Todd's cottage and The Toll Bar House on Pool Bank. In fact, if you shield your eyes from the sun and look up across the fields half a mile back to Pool Bank, the other shelter can clearly be seen perched on the hillside.

Inscribed in stone inside the lower shelter are the words "Presented to Pool Parish Council by Holmes and William Whiteley 1955". A nice gesture by the owners of the nearby historic paper mill so that their workers might not have to stand out in the rain after finishing a twelve-hour shift.

After the long slog up Leeds Road out of Otley then the descent down Old Pool Bank Road it will be a joy to be on level ground for the rest of the walk back into Otley. As you continue, the massive red brick structure of Pool Paper Mills or Whiteley's Mill comes into view.

The Whiteley family originated in the Halifax neighbourhood, where William Whiteley built a paper mill at Barkisland in 1866. He subsequently moved to Horsforth and then to Skyreholme, near Appletreewick, in 1875. In 1886, his three sons set up on their own at Pool-in-Wharfedale. Initially, the business specialised in pressboards for the textile industry and developed into the production of insulating boards and papers for the electrical trades. "Elephantide" insulating board was its most successful product and by 1936, the mill at Pool had become the largest pressboard factory in the world. The business was incorporated as a private company in 1920 and went public in 1946. It was acquired by Swiss interests in 1981.

The Whiteley family were major local employers throughout most of the 20th century and were responsible for building some fine workers' cottages and almshouses in the 1930s which are now within the conservation area of Pool-in-Wharfedale. Part of the original Whiteleys Mill site now houses a local brewery, a cloth weaving company, and an engineering company and as such is still busy today.

Heading along Pool Road towards Otley, you pass by various houses that once accommodated managers and the like from the nearby mill. Here you can take a look at the swollen river Wharfe as it passes over the huge weir just beyond the trees. To do this you must duck through the trees opposite the lodge for the Caley Hall Estate and struggle through the undergrowth towards the river edge. The original weir which stood behind The Blue Barn animal feed store was tiny in comparison to this massive swirling entity of white water that now stands before you.

The smaller and older weir was constructed to power what was known as Walk Mill or High Mill. This mill was used to produce paper, woollen, and leather products at various times in its life, and has been described in the Otley Parish Register as being partially swept away in September 1673. It was owned by the Fawkes family of Farnley Hall until sold to the Whiteley family in 1920. The larger paper mill appears to have been originally built by the farmer and maltster John Milthorp around 1762 and later sold to Michael Nicholson in 1808.

It was then let to the brothers Ben, Sam and William Whiteley in 1886, William eventually bought the mill in 1918 from Leeds Corporation Waterworks. The business was bought by the Swiss company Weidmann in 1981 who invested heavily and production continues today.

Return to the road after a few minutes and continue towards Otley for a few metres till you reach the old Pool Road. This old track is only eight hundred metres in length and winds around a large body of water where Anglers reign supreme and dog walkers are frowned upon. The new Pool Road cut this whole corner off when it was built.

Heading towards Otley you will approach the cemetery opposite the former Summercross pub. It is here that the tragic Elizabeth Todd is buried. It seems that most of Otley's good and great also reside in this sacred spot. Here you may notice many of the familiar small white headstones of the war dead. Always so young yet lying in silence beside old Wharfedale folk who lived to be a hundred or more.

As you head into Otley to end this walk you pass the Cross Green home of Otley Rugby Union Club and from here it is only a short distance back to the town centre where you can end this walk and catch a bus onto further destinations.

Thorner to Wike Via Pompocali

Thorner is reached by the 840, 843 Yorkshire Coastliner bus or the number 7 Transdev bus. The approximate distance for this walk is 4.5 miles.

Military deception is as old as military action itself. Hannibal, widely recognised as one of the finest military commanders in history, made extensive use of deception in his campaigns. The Ancient Greeks were noted for several forms of tactical deception and they certainly invented smoke screens during the Peloponnesian War and later stories refer to the famous Trojan horse which allowed them to defeat Troy.

Misinformation and visual deception was employed during World War I and came into even greater prominence during World War II with the Starfish sites employed by the British Government. This particular historical walk on the Eastern side of Leeds is one of two within this book that allows you to visit a former Starfish site.

This walk commences in Thorner where the bus conveniently deposits you in the village centre. Here, there is archaeological evidence of Bronze Age and Anglo-Saxon settlements, while the name St Osyth's Well, just West of the church, refers to a Viking Age saint.

The village appears in the 1086 Domesday Book as "Torneure" which means "thorn bank". The ancient parish of Thorner covered 4400 acres in the wapentake of Skyrack in the West Riding of Yorkshire. The parish included the townships of Scarcroft and Shadwell, which became separate civil parishes in 1866.

In 1245 the village acquired a market, and the area around Main Street shows a typical Medieval layout of strips leading from a market street. The base of a medieval market cross is on Butts Garth. As well as farming, pottery was a local industry in the Middle Ages, supplanted by the textile industry in the 18th and 19th centuries. The village church of St Peter is built in the later English Gothic style and has a square embattled tower. In the graveyard is the grave of John Philips, who lived to be 118 years of age.

The first port of call is to visit the only remaining building on the local Starfish site that once helped protect the city of Leeds from the Luftwaffe. From the village centre you head up Stead Lane and after passing a clutch of quaint old cottages, you reach the remaining abutment of the bridge that once carried the Leeds to Wetherby railway line. Nearby are two substantial Victorian houses on a lane named Spion Kop which gives an indication of the hilly nature of the local topography. The Battle of Spion Kop in South Africa was fought in 1900 on the largest hill in the region. It was popular at the time to name many football terraces 'Spion kop' when they were made out of huge mounds of earth banking.

Here the pasture opens up and the hedgerows become sentinels that guard the approaches to the Starfish site. The flat, level and expansive fields are roughly seven miles from Leeds city centre and it was here where the Thorner Starfish site was situated.

Starfish sites were large-scale night-time decoys created during the Blitz to simulate burning British cities. The aim was to divert German night bombers from their intended targets so they would drop their ordnance over the countryside. The sites were constructed around four to six miles from their protection target and at least one mile from any other settlement. They consisted of elaborate light arrays and fires, controlled from a nearby bunker and laid out to simulate a fire-bombed town.

By the end of the war, there were 237 decoys protecting 81 towns and cities around the country. The only remaining sign of the Starfish site at Thorner is the red brick control bunker. This stands just off Ellercar Lane with the actual fire decoys being spread around the adjoining fields. The lofty vantage point of the starfish site would ensure the blazing fires would be seen for miles around.

The decoy crews had a very dangerous job, as they were effectively inviting the Luftwaffe to blow them sky-high, and these bunkers were their only real protection. The bunker had a blast wall built in front of the entrance point and was buried under soil for more added protection.

Decoy sites, like airfields, were constructed to appear as realistic as possible during daylight attacks, but the decoy bomb sites only needed to look convincing at night. In reality, the blazing towns were ingenious contraptions of fire baskets, scaffolding, tanks and troughs. Fire baskets were set out in patterns over the site, flare cans topped up with creosote were placed inside. They also utilised what was known as fire boilers. These were large tanks that were fixed on top of scaffolding with pipes leading via a toilet type cistern to a long trough. One tank was filled with oil, the other with water. Inside each trough was a wick containing the electrically fired detonator that would initially set light to the oil content.

Once the oil was burning, cisterns on the tanks would allow alternate flushes of oil and water to run into the trough, giving an explosion of fire, very much like someone putting out a large frying pan fire with water. Flames would shoot into the air and create an impressive illusion of a burning city below. The hoodwinked Luftwaffe would then drop their bombs on a few old empty fields before flying off home. Deceiving the Germans must have felt so good to the men that operated the Starfish sites.

Leaving the site you must retrace your steps back along Ellercar Lane towards the village of Thorner once again. Passing by St. Peters Church you move along Church View and in a few moments will come to the junction with Milner Lane. Here on the junction stands a marvellous pair of early eighteenth-century cottages. Each mullioned window has a wooden shutter at each side. These simple wood panels contain a knights cross that has been carved into the wood.

Across from the junction is the beginning of a section of what remains of a Roman road which runs to Scarcroft and beyond to Wigton Moor Whin. This route was only one of numerous examples of Roman activity in this area. Not far away is a place that is reputed to be the site of a Roman quarry called Pompocali and its attendant spoil heaps. Although the heaps are covered in grass it does appear to have a "lunar-like" landscape if you use a little imagination……honest.

Milner Lane leaves the village along a slight shelf above the site of the long-gone railway station. Gentle woodland on one side and open fields on the other line this lane as it snakes its way towards Scarcroft Hall. This section of the walk imparts something of a pastoral feeling I as you stride along this most quintessential of English country lanes.

Passing by Scarcroft Hall on your left, it is less than a mile to the country path that takes you down the hill to Pompocali. Care and attention must be paid here as the track down to Pompocali and beyond to Scarcroft village is easy to miss. No more than a simple gate at the head of a small track down through the woods it belies its importance. The track itself runs along the line of another ancient Roman road, crosses Bardsey Beck via a footbridge then rises up the hill towards Scarcroft.

The edge of Hetchell Wood stands alongside the track with thick hedgerows on the other side. It has the effect of hemming you in and funnelled you downhill towards Pompocali. The hedgerows melt away to reveal the sprawling open pastureland once again with thick patches of wild Garlic throwing their well-defined aroma around as you pass by.

Here, depending on the season, will be a carpet of wild flowers including wood anemones, celandines, violets and Bluebells in flower. The gap in the hedgerow presents you with your first view of Pompocali as the huge grass-covered spoil heaps rise from the hillside below you. The mysterious and ethereal Pompocali lies between two ancient Roman roads on the edge of Hetchell Wood. This site is an archaeological enigma.

It is the remains of an ancient quarry, that much is known, but who built it and why they piled the spoils in such a peculiar manner is unknown. The spoils are not simply placed in heaps but laid out with a curiously stepped Ziggurat formation.

It is likely the site was used in Roman times as the footpath I used to gain access is the remains of the Roman Road. The fact that a Roman altar was found in the stream nearby and the only known Roman villas in the area were about a mile away also indicates an important site for the Romans and as the roads specifically converge there, it must have held some significance to them.

The hillocks are probably the equivalent of coal mine slag heaps - the useless material from the quarrying at nearby Hetchell Crag. Although there is no absolute concrete evidence that this was a Roman site the general consensus of opinion states that it most likely is. It is easy to imagine Mediterranean men far from home beavering away creating these silky slopes.

On the edge of Pompocali lies Bardsey Beck. Here, this age-old watercourse runs along the bottom of the small valley and it is shallow enough to have been used as a ford in ancient times. Today it is crossed by a wooden footbridge before the track leads over the old Wetherby and Leeds railway line and up the hill towards Scarcroft. This simple dirt track leads upwards through three fields until it reaches Wetherby Road.

Once you reach this point you have to open your stride and head along Wetherby Road in the general direction of Leeds. Passing by Syke Lane and its fine old Malthouse, you must once again be on the lookout for a simple gate across a simple country track. Passing by the fine Victorian houses of Marlborough House and Beaconsfield Villas, you will find the track on your right at the side of a small garage and car repair workshop directly opposite Scarcroft Grange

This track is actually a continuation of the Roman track that you have followed from the far side of Pompocali. Once again its appearance belies its significance as the track leads you alongside the southern boundary of the large garden of Beacon House in an area named Black Moor.

Here on the south-eastern corner of the garden once stood a tiny humble cottage named Ivy Cottage. Sadly this evocatively named abode is no more but the footprint can still be seen faintly on the hard ground.

From here it is something of a long haul along Tarn Lane towards Brandon Ings and Wigton Moor Whin. The landscape is open, vivid and flat and is the kind of landscape where you can see for miles. The Roman road surfaces once again at the far end of Tarn lane and as you near the end of this road the gentle thwack of golf balls in the middle distance tells you that Alwoodley Golf Course is close by.

According to the old maps, the Roman road or track that you have been following for most of the day continues across the green of the Alwoodley Golf course. When you arrive at the course boundary you must walk through the plantation of woodland that runs through the centre of the course.

The well-defined path and evidence of woodland husbandry throughout the wood tells you that this was a working area. After perhaps ten minutes of meandering through the swathes of spring Bluebells you will arrive at the rear of a collection of small buildings. A path leads around the side and out into a gravel courtyard, and this you must cross to continue along the track towards the club entrance.

From this point it is but a short walk to Harrogate Road from where you can catch the bus back to Leeds to complete your journey.

To commence this walk you must catch the 526 Yorkshire Tiger bus from central Queensbury towards the village of Bradshaw. Queensbury itself is reached by taking the 576 bus from either Halifax or Bradford. Alternatively you can walk from Queensbury and this will add one mile to the distance of this walk. The approximate distance of this walk is 5.6 miles.

Upon reaching The Queen's Head (formally named The Raggalds) pub you must exit the bus and begin the walk up Perseverance Lane towards Soil Hill which looms in the distance directly opposite.

The object on this road that everyone notices is a monument stone that stands on the right side after two hundred yards. It commemorates the opening of the road in November 1871 as prior to that date the road was unmade and fully deserved its nickname of "Mucky loin"(lane). This road had long been problematic in winter as water from the moorland above caused rutting down past the row of cottages. At the bottom, the fields were often flooded, and hence the road too.

The residents of the adjacent houses and farms clubbed together to finance the construction (£75) of the road but it took so long that it was named "Perseverance" Road when it was finally completed.

The residents provided the labour themselves to save on the construction costs. Today the road appears quite civilised but its long straight rise does give you an indication of how tiresome it would have been to transverse in the days before the modern construction.

After passing the farmhouse of Small Tail and its adjacent roadside cottages, the road turns left and skirts along the side of Soil Hill. At 1300 feet above sea level Soil Hill or Swilling Hill (to use its ancient name) is the highest point in the Queensbury and surrounding area and naturally affords views that can only be dreamt about.

On this stretch of road are the properties of Sun Farm, Millers Row and Cloth Row or Hall as it is known today. Sun Farm was formally known as "Charnocks" after the family who occupied it in the seventeenth century. From the early eighteenth century to 1906 there was a Beer House at the farm. This was originally named The Gin Pit and latterly The (Rising) Sun. Its time of glory was perhaps in 1803 when it was chosen as a beacon site in case of invasion by Napoleon.

As you pass these properties you must be on the lookout for a track that leads off the road to the right, past a covered reservoir and up towards the summit of Soil Hill. Once you have traversed a cattle grid set in the track you will see one of the few complete Dew Ponds not just in this area but in any area.

The Dew Pond is only a few feet away to your left and, surrounded by its defence of small standing stones, it stands out in this somewhat barren landscape. The flat stones are arranged in such a way as to preclude larger beasts such as cattle from entering the pond and destroying the bottom layer therefore allowing the captured moisture to dissipate. Smaller animals like Sheep can access the water through the narrow entry point.

A Dew Pond is a small artificial body of water usually sited on the top of a hill which is intended for watering livestock. Dew ponds are used in areas where a natural supply of surface water may not be readily available. They are usually shallow, saucer-shaped and lined with puddled clay, chalk or marl on an insulating straw layer over a bottom layer of chalk or lime.

To deter earthworms from their natural tendency of burrowing upwards, which in a short while would make the clay lining porous, a layer of soot would be incorporated or lime mixed with the clay.

The clay is usually covered with straw to prevent cracking by the sun and a final layer of chalk rubble or broken stone to protect the lining from the hoofs of sheep or cattle. It is one of the few remaining Dew Ponds that remain in a complete condition with surrounding stones anywhere around these parts.

This area of Soil Hill is popular with bird watchers or "Twitchers" as they are known. The air will be still and silent and this only serves to enhance the feeling of isolation. From here you will be able to clearly make out the far-away shape of Idle Hill in the distance. The massive chimney of Listers Mill in Manningham is also visible as is Salts Mill in Saltaire.

It is said that on a clear day no less than three of England's National Parks are visible from here. The Peak District to the South, the Yorkshire Dales to the North and in the very far distance The Hambleton Hills on the edge of the North Yorkshire Moors.

Between the sixteenth and nineteenth centuries, Soil hill was one of the busiest coal mining areas in the Halifax coal bed. The circular remains of the tops of the old pit shafts are still visible on its slopes. The coal was near to the surface and provided a ready supply to the local industries.

Another of Soil Hill's greatest virtues was the certain type of clay that laid underneath the soil and top turf along its summit. This substance was ideal for making pottery amongst other things and the last remaining Potter working from the Kilnworks down on the Ogden side was a man named Isaac Button. To reach this point you must slowly traverse down the Eastern side of Soil Hill.

Built around 1900, this brick building with a Welsh slate roof runs east-west adjacent to east end at the top of the hill slope. Within the western part was a bottle kiln with internal radial walls and six segment- arched fire holes around the perimeter. Four flues from beneath the kiln floor run up the hill to the square chimney. Two of these heated the drying shed adjacent to the kiln and two heated a parallel pent-roofed shed where clay slurry was dried before forming. This method of firing and ventilation and the use of waste heat to dry slurry represent an important innovation in earthenware manufacture.

Issac Button was one of the last true English Country Potters and he was renowned for making a ton of clay pots in any 1 day. In fact, he was once timed from throwing the lump of clay onto the potter's wheel, producing an excellent pot and then cutting it off using a wire cutter which in total took him 22 seconds. This would translate into 120 pots in any one hour and up to 1200 in any one day.

By 1900 England had only around one hundred country potteries and sadly by the end of the depression no more than a dozen. At Soil Hill there had been a pottery facility since the 17th century and before the First World War this pottery shop employed thirteen men. As time passed, Mr Button ended up working the pottery business on his own because he could not find anyone to take an apprenticeship with him. He passed eighteen years working there on his own.

In the past this side of Soil Hill will have been a veritable hive of activity with old Isaac amongst others throwing his shapes onto the rapidly spinning potter's wheel. Looking down the hillside at the now dilapidated pottery works it is easy to imagine Isaac weighing out the clay using a large set of scales. He shapes it into one small ball and one large ball. He lifts a large vat from one side of the workshop to the other.

Making a base out of the small ball of clay on the wheel, he places the larger ball on top and begins to mould it into a vat, smoothing the edges with the card and making a funnel at the top. He then cuts the vat from the wheel with wire and uses a crescent bracket to help him lift it to the workbench.

Large pots with handles are lined up on the shelves in the kiln. Isaac breaks pieces of clay into smaller sausage shapes, and with the slip, places the pieces of clay onto either side of a finished pot. He shapes them over the top to create a handle.

Leaving behind the ghost of Issac Button you pass banks of heather along Coal Lane and before long arrive at Halifax Road. From here you must cross the road and make your way over the fields towards the majestic body of water known as Ogden Reservoir. Find the track that leads you to New Moss Farm, where you join the short remains of a Roman road as it shoots like the proverbial arrow across the fields towards the heavy woodland that surrounds Ogden Reservoir.

The moss-covered ruins of a long-gone cottage named Spring Head can still be clearly be seen amongst the mature trees that populate this section of the woodland. Here things change in the woods as the loud excited screams and laughs of families enjoying the wonderful natural surroundings shatter the silence. Distant dogs bark excitedly as they run the many trails that pervade this entire area.

Ogden Water itself is a 34.5-acre reservoir surrounded by 174 acres of mixed mature woodland and open moor. The construction of the reservoir commenced in 1854 by the Halifax Corporation to augment the general water supply to the town. This scheme employed five hundred men and took until 1858 to complete. Holding nearly 222,000,000 gallons of water and standing over three hundred metres above sea level the reservoir is capable of supplying the needs of the town by gravity alone.

The woodlands that surround the reservoir were planted in 1905 with some planting and felling around WW2. The dominant tree in the woodland is Scots Pine, with Larch, Sycamore, Beech and Silver Birch also commonplace. Many people have visited this place over the years and a fair few have had benches placed around the water's edge inscribed with their names in remembrance after they had died. This is fairly commonplace around the many scenic reservoirs in the West Yorkshire area.

As you approach the concrete embankment at the far side you may catch a faint whiff of freshly brewed coffee in the air. That, along with the aroma of freshly baked bread and cut grass are surely amongst the most heavenly of smells a man's nose can detect. The smell can only be coming from a small café and shop on the far side of the embankment and it is here that you may choose to head to quench your thirst and take a rest for a while.

After suitable refreshment you must once again walk across the large embankment to the far side and turn left along a small footpath that skirts along the side of Black Hill. Her a few isolated cottages lay sprinkled across the far side of the ravine and a busy mill stream winds its way along the bottom.

Evidence of the former textile industry can be found along many streams and becks in Calderdale. This particular stream fed the workings of one such mill named Bottoms Mill. This was a Worsted spinning mill dating from the early 1800s. Though now overgrown, it provides a good example of the feature necessary to power a mill by water.

The embankment across the stream created a dam giving control over the water flow. The position of the wooden Goit, which fed the water wheel, and the position of the former wheel are still visible down in the bottom of the ravine.

After perhaps twenty minutes walking you will eventually surface on the pristine carpet like putting green of Halifax Golf Club. This course was created in 1901 in response to a rise in popularity in the game of Golf around this time. The clubhouse was built on the site of some old cottages in 1902 and the course soon extended from nine holes to a full nineteen holes.

After exiting the clubhouse car park you turn left and take Union Lane which in turn leads to Rocks Lane, and before long you pass the hamlet of Lower Brockholes on the way towards Mixenden. At the end of Rocks Lane turn left along Lane Head Lane until you reach the junction with White Gate. Here the junction is flanked by Upton House on one side and Rose View on the other. Here on the right you will walk along a cobbled pavement and pass the houses of Cock Pit and Shaking House before arriving at the head of a further walled cobbled pathway leading down towards Mixenden on your right.

The name Mixenden derives from the Anglo Saxon 'mixen' (compost or dung heap) and 'den' which usually refers to pasture land, usually for pigs. In the 15th / 16th century, there were tales of a buried treasure hoard at Hunter Hill but an expedition in 1510 failed to find anything. The treasure-hunters – who hailed from Bingley – were said to have used black magic to find the hoard. When the church heard about this, the men were forced to do penance at local fairs.

The walled cobbled footpath leads you onto Mill Lane. After a few hundred yards Hays lane leads off to the right. Hays Lane was the site of the famous Mixenden riot, where, in 1896, a young man called Varley was charged with raping Sarah Ann – daughter of engine tenter Peter Webster of Hey's Lane, Mixenden. He was sentenced to seven years' imprisonment.

On the evening of Wednesday, 5th August 1896, a group of locals who knew the man and the girl – and her reputation – protested at the sentence, and stormed the girl's home, throwing tin cans and stones at the house. Webster and his four sons were afraid to leave the house to fetch the police. The girl and her mother hid in the cellar as windows were smashed and the house damaged.

Several people were charged with riotously and tumultuously assembling and doing damage to the house of Sophia and Peter Webster:

Fred Rushworth [aged 20] (butcher) - sentenced to 3 months' imprisonment

Herbert Ambler [aged 24] (clogger) - sentenced to 4 months' imprisonment

Arthur Crabtree [aged 28] (delver) - who was found not guilty

John Horsfield [aged 17] (overlooker) - sentenced to 3 months' imprisonment

Tom Heap [aged 22] (carter) - sentenced to 3 months' imprisonment

Willie Skelton [aged 28] (delver) - who was found not guilty

Jonathan Clayton [aged 30] (delver) - charges against him were withdrawn

After the incident, the Websters moved to Morley and nothing was ever heard from them again.

The village of Mixenden had its own Corn Mill of course. This manorial corn mill, mentioned in 1492 and like the Wheatley Corn Mill, belonged to the Savile family. It stood on the Halifax side of Mixenden Bridge and the entrance gates still remain. It was used by the Sutcliffe and Priestley families and other owners and tenants have included William Walsh in 1845, Bairstow Brothers [1845-1898], and William Simpson in 1861.

When you reach the junction with Clough Lane you will have come to the end of this particular historical walk. From here you can catch the bus into Halifax and from there onto any further destination to suit your particular needs.

To reach Greengates you can catch a number of local buses from Bradford interchange namely the 645: (First Bradford) Buttershaw - Greengates via Five Lane Ends and Bradford City Centre, 35: (First Leeds) Leeds - Kirkstall - Greengates - Thorpe Edge, 60: (Keighley Bus Company) Leeds - Keighley via Bingley and Saltaire, 747: (Flying Tiger) [Airport Direct] Bradford - Leeds Bradford Airport – Harrogate.

This walk begins at Greengates war memorial which stands on the junction of the former Dudley Hill, Killinghall and Harewood Trust Turnpike Road and New Line. Today this long stretch of road is known as Harrogate Road and as its name suggests runs all the way to the North Yorkshire spa town of the same name.

From the war memorial you follow Harrogate Road downhill towards Apperley Bridge, passing the Yorkshire Eye Hospital on the left and the large Anglican church dedicated to St. John the Evangelist on the right. As you approach the Dog and Gun public house you will be in the area known due to its profusion of Dye Houses as, strangely enough, Dyehouse Fold.

It was common in former times for the mills of Bradford to be grouped in the same vicinity according to their purposes, and following this trend the mills adjacent to the canal at Apperley Bridge were predominantly used for the dyeing of wool and cloth. This area between the mills and the New Line road at Greengates was used for "Tenterhooking", and one of the streets of the new build estate on the site pays homage to this former use with the name Tenterfield.

Tenterhooks are hooks in a device called a tenter. Tenters were originally large wooden frames which were used as far back as the 14th century in the process of making woollen cloth. After a piece of cloth was woven, it still contained oil from the fleece and some dirt. A craftsperson called a fuller or waulker cleaned the woollen cloth in a fulling mill, and then had to dry it carefully or the woollen fabric would shrink. To prevent this shrinkage, the fuller would place the wet cloth on a tenter, and leave it to dry outdoors.

The lengths of wet cloth were stretched on the tenter (from Latin tendere, meaning "to stretch") using tenterhooks (hooked nails driven through the wood) all around the perimeter of the frame to which the cloth's edges were fixed, so that as it dried the cloth would retain its shape and size. In some manufacturing areas like this one at Greengates, entire tenter-fields were once a common sight.

Continuing on Harrogate Road, you now cross over the river using the bridge constructed in 1936 to augment the original bridge (1777), which still survives a few metres to the west. Here to the east during the Football season Bradford City train on fields which are often waterlogged in the winter.

This area was also the site of Bradford's first and so far only Aerodrome in the early years of the 20th century. Suppressing the lure of a well-kept pint of ale at The Stansfield Arms you stay on Harrogate Road heading up something of a gentle gradient.

Built as a Coaching Inn in the style of a farmhouse and barn and dating back to 1543, The Stansfield Arms once housed the soldiers commanded by Lord Halifax as they waited to cross the nearby river Aire en route for Leeds during the English Civil War. The beamed historical public house with its vintage wooden floors was also used as a gatehouse for the nearby Stansfield Estate at Esholt. The Minstrels Gallery in the old part of the building is a delight to behold and one of the few surviving examples in West Yorkshire.

Harrogate Road now becomes Apperley Lane as it starts its climb up the valley side in the direction of Rawdon and Little London. Carrying on up the incline you pass the lodge of Woodhouse Grove School and the grade II listed Wesleyan Methodist church before turning right along Woodlands Drive. Here lies the location of the original Apperley Bridge railway station, which was finally closed by the British Railways Board, as a result of the Beeching Axe, at about 9.30 pm on 20 March 1965.

The Leeds and Bradford Railway opened on 30 June 1846. At first, there were no intermediate stations, such had been the haste to get the line opened. Temporary stations were quickly provided, including Apperley Bridge, which opened sometime during July 1846. A permanent structure followed about a year later. It comprised two platforms, partly covered by an overall roof.

The main building ran parallel to the railway on the south side up at road level. A principal customer of the station was Woodhouse Grove School, whose land had been crossed by the Railway. In 1849 the Railway agreed to purchase gas from the school in order to light the station. The Railway was widened to four tracks circa 1900, taking more land from Woodhouse Grove School in the process. The school used the money to build a new swimming pool. The station was enlarged to four platforms, with a distinctive wooden building above at road level. The original station building was swept away when the cutting was widened to accommodate the new "fast lines" on the south side.

From here you continue along Woodlands Drive which will take you up the valley side towards Cragg Wood. This area covers a rural suburb of fine Victorian Villas set in spacious wooded grounds which was developed in the 1850s. The surviving woodlands of the area and the vernacular buildings of the farmsteads and cottages recall an earlier landscape.

You are now walking along the former carriage drive of the estate across the contours of the valley as it continues to rise up towards Rawdon and Little London. Here you can look back across the open fields and meadows below you as the carriage drive takes you past substantial Victorian mansions commissioned by the wealthy industrialists of the growing nearby city of Bradford.

Views of the villas are limited from the roadside as they are set back in private grounds surrounded by mature trees of all descriptions, but their elaborate gateways and lodges act as focal points as you walk along. These Victorian mansion houses feature high walls of architectural ornamentation in the Gothic Revival, Tudor and Elizabethan styles. The high-quality materials used in the construction included local Gritstone and squared and coursed masonry. These magnificent houses of the wealthy were built on the varying terraces on the valley side, allowing each to benefit from the open views across the valley.

At the junction with Cragg Wood Drive, you need to find a tiny footpath which is flanked by massive stone walls that ran along the edge of the grounds of Buckstone Hall. This path had something of a tunnel-like appearance as the walls were themselves topped by the overhanging branches of the mature trees which lined the grounds of this fine house. Designed by the Bradford Architects Lockwood and Mawson for Herbert Dewhirst, Buckstone Hall was nicknamed "Little Windsor "or "The Castle" due to its dominant tower which was clearly visible for miles around.

The Dewhirst family lived here until 1911 when the property was sold to Sir Arthur Croft of The Thornbury Engineering Company. The house became a casino noted locally for its late-night gambling in the 1960s.

Walking along Cliffe Drive, you pass by the houses of Crag Head and Daisy Hill. The superb mansion of Daisy Hill was owned and occupied in the 1860s by Henry Brown, the Mayor of Bradford and co-owner of the well-known store Brown Muff and Co. Two hundred yards past Daisy Hill you take yet another footpath which will guide you towards Buckstone House. From this point if you glance back down the valley and may just about see the outline of the mansion named Summer Hill. This fine Victorian Gothic revival residence was at one time occupied by William Henry Salt, the Second Baronet and eldest Son of Sir Titus Salt.

Today Buckstone House is known as Apperley Grange. Now the location of Rawdon Golf Club, Apperley Grange is situated one hundred and fifty yards from "Buckstones Rock". This rock is a significant local landmark and is thought to have been the secret meeting place for 17th century Baptists and other none conformists in the area before their chapel was built a short distance away. The famous Preacher John Wesley was reputed to have preached here on a number of occasions.

This whole area gives an idea of the wealth and privilege that the Victorian industrialists enjoyed. The estate was a forerunner of what the aborted estate of a similar nature across the valley at Calverley was to have been. You may be used to seeing and admiring the humble cottages and farms across the Bradford area during your rambles, but now you are walking amongst the former grand residences of their wealthy paymasters.

Carrying on the footpath you quickly pass by Kent House. This house was once owned by the Granage family who lost a Son at the Battle of Arras in World War One. Lieutenant William Briggs Granage of 235th Brigade of The Royal Field Artillery died of his wounds aged 37 on the 14th May 1917. He was killed by a shell as he walked to the headquarters of an infantry brigade near Swan Chateau and was buried in Lijssenthcek Military Cemetery.

Now you will be approaching Little London, and here you cross Micklefield Lane and continue to walk along London Lane to once again be amongst streets of humble old cottages. The designated conservation area of Little London occupies a spur of high ground in a somewhat dramatic position above the Aire valley. Cragg Wood tumbles down to the south and to the west can be found the Esholt estate. To the north-east the land rises gradually and culminates in nearby Billing Hill and the moors above Yeadon.

Little London probably originated as a small farmstead but quickly grew into the form we see today in the late 18th and early 19th centuries. This was largely due to the local weaving industry. Here the streets are narrow and the cottages gathered close together as you pass by The Princess public house to cross Apperley Lane. Here you can take a small lane which takes you across open fields and down towards the Esholt estate.

Here at the head of the tiny lane stands the oldest house in the Little London area. Lane Head House dates from the early 18th century (1710-20) and is thought to have been built as a steward's house that was connected to the Esholt estate. The former service cottages to the house also survive as do Smithy Hill cottages (1750), The Grove (1797) and The Folly (late 18th century).

The small track leads you down the valley side past huge allotments filled with just about every vegetable you can imagine. Down at the valley bottom you can see the railway line and from here you can skirt alongside it to the east for a while to arrive at a substantial stone bridge.

This ancient packhorse trail from Rawdon to Esholt is steep and narrow in the extreme and the remaining setts were uneven and troublesome due to the wear from the many horses and humans who had walked it over the centuries.

As you near the railway line the trail turns sharply to the right before disappearing into a thickly wooded area that flanks the line. The railway bridge stands upon Gill Lane and this track leads into the Esholt sewage plant. Even though you are still quite a distance from there the smell could be troublesome depending on the wind direction. Try not to think of the nature of what is stirring around in the tanks and filter beds as you continue along Gill Lane in the wooded area that flanks it.

The tiny beck of Yeadon Gill runs alongside you now in a gully as you walk down the track towards the junction with The Avenue. Turning left here you take this wide modern open road for a short distance before turning off along Coronation Avenue. This road leads straight through the centre of the sewage plant like a dagger through the heart and officially you perhaps should not be going this way.

The only other alternative is to take the long way round and cross the river Aire by way of the small iron footbridge some distance away. This, in turn, will bring you out near Bottom Farm and Thackley Canal Bridge. At this point you will pass by what was known as the Press House.

The official name for the Press House was the Sludge Disposal Building and inside here were 128 steam filter presses which compressed sludge to recover grease (lanolin) which was used for a variety of applications. The pressed residue was sold as fertiliser to meet the cost of operating the plant. After Bradford's woollen textile industry declined, the Press House became roofless and derelict.

Now you cross the turn bridge to start the walk up Ainsbury Avenue which would take you to Thackley. At the far end of Ainsbury Avenue is the site of a former open-air school with some surviving ruins which indicate its former use.

In the years between 1908 and 1939, sickly children from the dense working-class areas of Bradford were brought in from the city centre to attend this groundbreaking school. In the early part of the 20th century Bradford's progressive education authority quickly saw that the open air, good food, and exercise would benefit the district's disadvantaged children.

These children of humble working-class parents normally lived in cramped conditions with poor sanitation. Bradford Council had recently bought Buck Wood as part of the land belonging to the Esholt Estate, which they needed for the development of their new sewage plant. Part of Buck Woods seemed ideal for the open-air school.

In 1908, 40 pupils were brought to the school by tram from the city centre to be fed and schooled in the south-facing open-fronted classrooms. Close to the main entrance to Buck Wood on Ainsbury Avenue is a plateau that was created from waste material from the first railway tunnel under the woods. This flat raised area was used as a playground by the children that attended the school, and foundations of some of the school buildings can still be seen leading down from the northeast edge of this plateau.

Soon after another row of chalet-style buildings was added which increased the number of available places to 120. By the time the school closed in 1939 thousands of children had benefitted from the special care and atmosphere offered by the school. During WWII, the buildings were used by the Army and the Home Guard. The raised plateau became the site for an anti-aircraft gun due to the area's proximity to the Avro aircraft factory at Yeadon. The buildings were finally burnt down in 1966 and most of the site cleared allowing it to return to nature.

Upon reaching the halfway point of Ainsbury Avenue you turn into Buck Woods through a large gate. After walking for only a few metres you will arrive at the raised plateau which was used as the playing field. Just to the side you may notice a set of stone steps leading down into the woods. Here you can walk down the twenty or so steps to emerge into a clearing in the trees where foundations for some of the school's buildings can be seen.

The locally cast bricks still lay in the soil as they have done for over a century. Tracing the outline of the open-fronted buildings it is easy to picture how they were arranged in the clearing. Standing there in the sun, the wood silent and still, it may be your imagination but you may hear the distant excited babble and chatter of children as they play their games on the plateau.

Filling their young lungs with the fresh air instead of the coal dust and smog of the inner city most would remember their days here with affection. From here it is only a short stroll into Thackley where this walk ends and you can catch the bus back into Bradford.

Blubberhouses

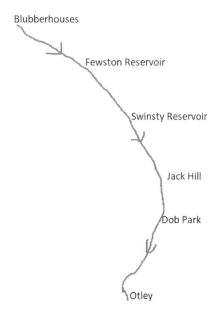

Fewston Reservoir

Swinsty Reservoir

Jack Hill

Dob Park

Otley

This walk is just about the most ambitious in terms of travelling by public transport of any within this guide. There is but one bus a day, and that is a Sunday or a Bank Holiday, from April through to September. Operated by Transdev Keighley, the 821 leaves from Keighley, Saltaire, Bingley, Shipley and Otley and will deposit you safely at Blubberhouses to commence this walk. The approximate distance for this walk is 8.0 miles

The bus will drop you outside the Anglican church of St. Andrew on the edge of Blubberhouses village. The name of the village derives from the Anglo-Saxon bluberhūs which means "the house(s) which is/are at the bubbling stream". From here you move through the tiny hamlet before crossing Blubberhouses bridge to continue along Hopper Lane in the direction of the Hopper Lane Hotel.

Here Hopper Lane becomes Skipton Road, which is a fast and extremely busy none pavement road so you must proceed with caution. After only a couple of minutes you will reach the point where you mustturn right away from the road onto a small track named Parkinson's Lane. This old packhorse trail will take you alongside Fewston Reservoir, onto the village of Fewston itself, before passing Swinsty Reservoir and then beyond through Dob Park and down the valley side into your final destination of Otley.

Parkinson's Lane is a simple woodland track which will lead you through the tightly packed thick woodland which, depending on the season, will present you will banks of Daffodils and Bluebells which are only broken by the entrances to two old redundant quarries. It may be hard to believe that there was once a sizable house named Crag Hall here, but sadly today no trace remains.

The mixed plantation contains trees such as Elder, Birch, and Sycamore which will try its best to disguise and hide the former sandstone quarries. These small quarries are evidence of the sheer resolve and endeavour of the men that made their living in them. Often worked by hand these wonderful documents to the past never fail to amaze due to their often remote locations.

After perhaps two miles or so the track changes to Busky Dike Lane but you still proceed past the densely packed woodland to one side and now open green fields on the other. Arriving at a clearing at the side of the road, you may notice the mound of moss covered stones that lay in a pile on your right. This is evidence that there was once a house here on this spot. Looking around the site I noticed what appeared to be a small underground storage room. Perhaps it was an icehouse as its semi-subterranean construction suggests its use was the preservation of food as well as storage.

Here you can clearly see Fewston Reservoir to your right. Constructed with a capacity of 3.5 million litres and situated in the charming Washburn valley, it shares an embankment with the smaller Swinsty Reservoir. The reservoir was built by the Leeds Waterworks Company under the management of Robert Brooks. The Consultants were Thomas Hawksley of Westminster and Edward Filliter of Leeds. Work began in 1874 and was completed in 1879.

Early in the work, Fewston Mill was demolished, as was West House Mill at Blubberhouses, with the stone going to build a wall around the reservoir. Continuing on with the reservoir on your right, you will now be approaching the village of Fewston and this is confirmed by the old village schoolhouse a little further along the lane on your left.

Today it is a private residence and your attention may be drawn to the rooftop stone bell housing. Containing only a thin slit in the stonework the bell itself would have been tiny but still big enough to be heard through the still air of this serene area.

But this magical area was once the scene of an influx of thousands of ghoulish sightseers which was denounced as revolting by the Rev F.M. Cubbon, the vicar of Fewston Parish Church. The reason why these morbid interlopers descended on the tiny village of Fewston was to creep around the churchyard and stand on tiptoe to peer through the windows of the village shop. The same village shop where Margaret Peel was bludgeoned to death 2nd March 1938.

The brutal murder left a dark cloud hanging over the village and is still remembered even today. The village shop was a four-roomed cottage selling sweets, tobacco, films and other items handy for villagers who had run out of goods between shopping trips to market at the towns of Otley or Harrogate. Margaret Peel lived there with her husband Jessie, a reservoir worker with Leeds Corporation, and their ten-year-old daughter also named Margaret.

The cottage was demolished fourteen months following the tragedy after serving the village as a store for nearly fifty years. The stone from the cottage was used to extend the nearby Post Office which took over the role of the village shop, a role which it still fulfils today. Some 250 metres after passing the school you will reach the junction with Back Lane, and if you turn left here, and walk a further 50 metres you will find yourself at the exact place where the village shop and murder site once stood. You are now standing on the very same spot on this tiny country lane where Margaret Peel was found with her brains splattered across the kitchen walls.

The interior of what was the cottage is now filled with dark green moss-covered rocks, wild nettles, and stones. In between these grow a number of tall and stout trees which block out most of the sunlight even in high summer. But the outline of the footprint of the cottage is still evident and easily seen despite the lack of available light on this strangely depressing spot.

A post-mortem showed that 37-year-old Mrs Peel had been struck eleven times on her head with the usual blunt instrument. She had been struck from behind leaving the strapping Daleswoman with no chance to defend herself. Reeling from the first blow she slumped with her head in the linen basket as the murderer proceeded to stove her head in. The body was found by a young local girl who alerted the Police, and they contacted the Vicar who drove the short distance to Swinsty Reservoir to break the bad news to the husband Jesse Peel.

Jesse told the Police that he had been at work on the reservoir when the crime was committed and the last time he saw his wife was when he kissed her goodbye that morning. Despite the lack of a motive and any real evidence, the Police charged Peel with the murder of his wife. The reservoir was dragged and after eight days the Police found a heavy tyre lever which they considered was the murder weapon. The lever had marks on it that suggested it might have come from a batch once owned by Jesse Peel's brother, who ran the Hopper Lane garage on the main road.

Of course, Peel denied any involvement in his wife's killing and pleaded not guilty at the trial. The trial, at Leeds Assizes before Lord Justice McGee, began on 10th May with the allegation that Peel had left his place of work at the reservoir and made his way home and killed his wife in a frenzy of violence. He then returned to the reservoir to resume work without being spotted. After retiring for only forty-two minutes, the jury returned a not guilty verdict and Jesse Peel left court a free man.

He never returned to the cottage that he had shared with his wife, and the Leeds Waterworks Committee, which owned the building, was unable to find another tenant to live in the cottage. Although he was cleared of the murder, a further cruel twist of fate was to rob Peel of the chance to rebuild his shattered life. Little more than five years after the shadow of the noose and the stain of infamy was lifted by the bland two-word statement by the jury foreman, Jesse Peel was killed in a road accident.

In August 1943 whilst cycling to work with the Home Guard, he collided with a car near to the murder site and died four days later from a fractured skull and shock. Gruesome and grisly murders occur in every town and city at some point in time, but as you stand on the site of Margaret Peel's murder, two thoughts may roll through your mind.

Firstly, how could the justice system place a man on trial for his life with no obvious motive and almost no evidence, and secondly how the hell could it happen in a place as beautiful as this?

Following this sobering experience you may seek some warm sun to chase away the murder blues, and so can continue along the lane through the hamlet of Fewston, past the church of St. Lawrence and The Grange to head for the causeway across the reservoir. Swinsty Reservoir can now clearly be seen to your right at this point.

Beneath the waters of the reservoir are the remains of New Hall, originally a home to the Fairfax family, whose members included Ferdinando Fairfax and the poet Edward Fairfax. Women in the nearby village of Timble were twice tried at York for witchcraft on the accusation of Edward, who suspected them of possessing his two daughters. Neighbouring Fewston Reservoir covers another Fairfax family home, Cragg Hall.

The reservoir was built by the Leeds Waterworks Company, and employed a labour force of around three hundred men under the management of Robert Brooks, previously an assistant at the construction of Lindley Wood Reservoir. The Consultants were once again Thomas Hawksley of Westminster and Edward Filliter of Leeds.

Work on the construction of the reservoir began in 1871. "The Huts", as they were known locally, were constructed to house the workforce, in part using materials from a water mill dismantled in the valley. The bulk of the materials for the dam itself came to Starbeck by rail. From there they were, at first, transported to the site using a steam traction engine pulling wagons. However, by 1872 this practice was put to an end due to the damage being caused to the 'Turnpike road', now the A59, and from then on materials were transported by contractors. At the site, a narrow-gauge railway was constructed, and two locomotives purchased, the first arriving in 1873 and the second in 1875.

The impact of the construction work was considerable for local residents, in ways both positive and negative. In his diaries, local man John Dickinson mentions the waterworks band coming with their music on Christmas Day, a visit to a "Magic Lantern performance at The Huts" and a waterworks sports day on Swinsty Moor with several hundred in attendance.

On the downside, he complains several times of "rough navvies" occupying the local inn at Timble, and expresses the hope they will soon be gone. As work neared completion in 1877, the huts were removed and the filling of the reservoir began. Work was finally completed in 1878.

On the banks of the reservoir stands Swinsty Hall, built in the 17th century. Local legend has it that the hall was built by a man named Robinson, who left nearby Fewston to seek his fortune in London. On arriving there, he found it in the grip of the great plague of 1603–4. Robinson took to looting the houses of the dead and amassed a great fortune with which he returned home, purchased the Swinsty estate, and built Swinsty Hall.

The truth appears more mundane – a family named Wood owned the Swinsty estates in the sixteenth century, and Francis Wood undertook to erect a new hall on the estate as part of a marriage contract. Unable to pay for it, he raised a loan from Henry Robinson, and when he got into further financial difficulties in 1590, Robinson foreclosed and took the hall and estates in lieu of the debt.

The hall was owned by a succession of Robinsons right up until 1772. At this point, the male Robinson line came to an end and the hall and estate passed to Robert Bramley, husband of Mary Robinson, and later his son John Bramley, and in 1853 John Bramley's son, also named John. Stone for the construction of Fewston Reservoir was purchased from the Swinsty Hall quarry in 1874, from a Mr Bramley.

At Swinsty, Picnickers and children will be enjoying the warm rays of the sun at the water's edge. They will most likely be totally oblivious to the macabre history of the nearby village and no doubt the ice cream from the enterprising van will taste extremely good.

After crossing the extended arm of Swinsty Reservoir via a concrete causeway, you will arrive at a small junction in the road. Here you must turn left to take Pinfold Lane. This quiet and leafy lane ambles alongside the shimmering water to guide you towards the embankment at the reservoir's end. After 250 metres the Pinfold in question is easy to spot on the right-hand side as most of the stone walls are still in situ. Sadly all Pinfolds are not that easy to spot.

A Pinfold was an animal pound where stray livestock such as pigs and sheep are impounded in a dedicated enclosure until claimed by their owners or sold to cover the costs of impounding. The area of both Fewston and Swinsty Reservoirs are very popular with day-trippers and countryside lovers due to the quite spectacular scenery. Here you may enjoy an overriding feeling of space and freedom as there appears to be plenty of room for all.

A further five hundred metres and you will be standing on the concrete embankment of Swinsty reservoir where you can view the huge overflow area below and the River Washburn as it snakes away towards Dob Park. From here you can follow the river until it reaches the magnificent old packhorse bridge on the ancient Monks trail at Dob Park a mile and a half away.

This small, civilised but important river gently winds its way along between lush green pastures and the slopes of Jack Hill. In spring flocks of sheep and their numerous newborn lambs will scatter and gambol before you as you trail along the valley floor. The Mother sheep will watch with beady eyes, ready to run again at the slightest rapid movement.

After a mile and a half you will reach the packhorse bridge that crosses the River Washburn at Norwood Bottom. From here the river flows into Lindley Reservoir. Constructed of Gritstone probably early in the seventeenth century with later eighteenth century repairs, this marvellous single-span bridge is paved with stone setts and flat blocks tied together with iron staples.

The bridge carried the trail from Dob Park Mill and Dob Park Lodge across the river to Norwood and Fewston and straddles the parish boundaries of Newall with Clifton and Weston. The bridge is built on the site of an ancient ford where the Monks would cross on their way to Otley and beyond. At this point there is a convenient wooden bench where you can sit, eat some food and rest whilst gazing over the smooth worn stones of the bridge and its path.

What stories this place could tell. Who had walked this way and where were they going. The trail of packhorses would wind their way down Jack Hill towards you. Each one would be led by a hooded Monk clad in a grey habit. The panniers were full and the horse's backs were piled high with fleeces. The gentle clip-clop of the hooves on the surface stone sett's would ring out around the valley floor as the procession reached the stone bridge.

Staring straight ahead the monks would be focused on keeping their charges in line and in control as a fully laden horse could shed its load in a second if spooked. The heavy breath from the dozen or so horse's nostrils gave testament to the sheer effort involved in descending down the hillside from Jack Hill. There was no rest for the wicked or indeed the good and pious as the track led instantly up the other side of the valley through Dob Park. On and up the valley side they plodded, slowly making their way towards the market in Otley to trade their woollen fleeces.

After a rest for suitable refreshment you may cross the bridge and start the climb up to Dob Park. The trail is winding and steep as it passes Dob Park Farm and it finally levels out right on the top. Here, if you look over to your right you will catch a glimpse of the relatively unknown Dob Park Hunting Lodge.

The ruins of the lodge stand almost forgotten on the windswept moorland of North Yorkshire. Originally one of three hunting lodges, this building would have provided a welcome respite from the scouring winds and the biting Yorkshire weather. At one time the lodge was occupied by a branch of the Vavasour family of Weston Hall, and during the Civil War it is said to have been shelled by Cromwell's soldiers.

The area is within the Royal Forest of Knaresborough, a former medieval hunting park, originally of William the Conquerer, and later John of Gaunt, the Duke of Lancaster. It is easy to imagine the people who would have gathered here for the past four hundred years, and the warmth that the stone walls would have provided in the deep mid-winter.

Passing by Dob Park House and Bride Cross House you soon reach the junction with Weston Moor Road and Newall Carr Road and continue along the later towards Otley. The road sweeps gently downhill as it dissects the lush green pasture between Weston Moor and Farnley Moor. In the distance The Chevin looms large above Otley to dominate the horizon, almost as if it was a God in the clouds watching over the subservient land below. The Chevin is Wharfedale and Wharfedale is The Chevin and each one would be nothing without the other.

Newall Carr Road continues to lead you past the occasional semi-isolated farmhouse and cottage until you reach the edge of the town of Otley. You may find yourself walking at quite a speed now as the road is on something of a gradient. You will soon pass The Roebuck Inn (or is it The Spite I've never been sure) and what remains of the old Otley Hospital.

After a few short minutes, you will be sat in Otley bus station waiting for the 653 bus to Bradford or perhaps to Menston Railway Station for a train home.

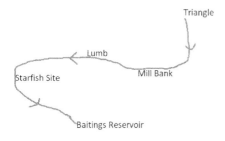

To begin this walk you need to catch the 560 bus from Halifax to Commons, or the X58 which will drop you most conveniently in the centre of the village of Triangle. The approximate distance for this walk is 4.7 miles.

Triangle is a village in Calderdale on the main A58 road over the Pennines near Halifax, and between Sowerby Bridge and Ripponden in the Ryburn valley. Historically part of the West Riding of Yorkshire, it dates mainly from the 19th century period of industrialisation but was here for some time prior. The name of the village derives from the patch of ground formed when the old road parted with the newer (A58) toll road to Rochdale. Previous to this time the village was named Pond.

You have to begin the ascent onto the moors by taking Oak Hill which very soon becomes Oak Lane. You will find this lane along the side of the long-closed former public house named The Triangle on the main road as it leaves the village. The inn was built around 1765 as a coaching inn for traffic on the triangle of land formed when the new turnpike was built. Here you may notice the tiny village war memorial which is attached to the gable end of the building.

Oak Lane climbs rather steeply past the farmhouses of Lower Deer Play and Deer Play before passing the former village slaughterhouse on your left. You are now on Mill Bank Road and after passing by Rawson Farm on your left you enter the village of Mill Bank.

Mill Bank is a Yorkshire in Bloom Gold award-winning village set in a conservation area. Its past is rooted in the cotton, woollen and silk industries. One hundred and fifty years ago the population was three times its current size and there were five local mills, seven pubs and a variety of shops, including one of the original Co-op shops which opened in the village in 1865.

Following a period of serious decline, the village was rescued from imminent demolition and designated as a conservation area in 1976. The village is on a steep south-facing valley with Lumb Beck, a fast-flowing stream that previously provided power for the mills, at the foot of the hill. There are old packhorse trails, ancient highways and many footpaths across the hillsides.

Physically, Mill Bank is a rather dispersed settlement with small stone cottages strung out along the roadside. As you pass through the village look for the fine former Methodist Chapel on your right and perhaps one of the areas finest surviving examples of a setted pave way running downwards to your left.

Upon leaving Mill Bank you head towards the tiny hamlet of Lumb. Soon the road changes to Lumb Lane and all along this road to your left runs the mill stream that once powered the forgotten Lumb Mill and further along Upper Lumb Mill. This deceptively powerful stream is now hidden by Great House Wood as it weaves its way down the valley floor towards Kebroyd.

Lumb Mill was a cotton mill which burned down on 15th October 1864 when it was occupied by Heal, Booth & Company (1859-1864) Upper Lumb Mill was a Fulling mill that was destroyed by fire on 15th January 1931. As you approach Cotton Stones, the lane narrows considerably before splitting as it passes over the stream. Here you may notice the two tiny stone bridges before continuing left along to the junction that lies only a few hundred yards ahead. The former mill pond for both aforementioned Lumb mills can still be seen across the road at this point.

You are now on Alma Lane and at the junction bare left along Clay Pits Lane. The house on the right of the junction is the former public house named The Alma. From here on the roadside workers cottages disappear as you begin to take to the open expanse of Flints Moor.

After only a few hundred yards turn right along Wicking Lane and pass silently by Hall Green, Hall Moor and Wicking Hall. Follow this track until you reach the site of the former Flints Reservoir. The dam of the reservoir is still there, but sheep graze the marshy bed where there was once water. It was possibly a mill reservoir as there was a mill at nearby Cotton Stones.

Wicking Lane has now ended and becomes no more than a moorland footpath. Continue along here until you reach a fork. Bear right to follow this track towards the ruin in the distance at Slate Delfs Hill. This was the control and operations bunker for a 'Starfish' decoy site intended to draw German bombers away from their intended target, in this case the railway station and yard at Greetland.

The decoy consisted of a double line of about a dozen flash pans, where oil would be burned to simulate incendiary bombs. There would also have been decoy lights and shadow buildings, possibly constructed using walling stone from alongside some of the enclosure period tracks in the area. The bunker consists of two rooms either side of a central entrance passage, defended by a high blast screen. The room on the right housed the generators. The control room was on the left, with an escape and observation hatch in the roof. The decoy itself was located to the south-west in the area leading towards Great Manshead Hill.

From here you head across the open expanse of moorland on any of the many footpaths towards the summit of Great Manshead Hill and its trig point. You now stand 1350 feet above sea level and from this lofty vantage point great views are afforded and you can literally see for miles even across to Manchester. Naturally the magnificent Baitings Reservoir can be seen down below you and it is in this direction that you must now travel.

Baitings Reservoir is a large water supply reservoir operated by Yorkshire Water close to Ripponden in the West Yorkshire Pennines. It lies in the valley of the River Ryburn and is the higher of two reservoirs built to supply Wakefield with water and was completed in 1956. The lower reservoir is named Ryburn Reservoir.

It was built upstream of Ryburn Reservoir in order to catch the water that was going to waste. A six mile long catchwater drain brings water to the dam from Cragg Vale. The reservoir was formally opened by the Wakefield Waterworks Committee on May 3rd 1957. The original stone bridge was submerged when the reservoir was filled and can be seen when the waters subside in times of drought. The cost of construction was £1,420,000.

During the construction of the reservoir there was one fatal accident that killed Thomas Straw Assistant Engineer, Kenneth Greatorex Signellor and Iwan Roghen, a Shotfirer and driller. All three were killed in the same blasting accident

From here it is all downhill so care must be taken not to turn an ankle in the occasionally rutted landscape. Once you reach Rochdale Road, which skirts along the northern edge of Baitings Reservoir, you can relax and rest awhile at the bus stop as you wait for the bus from Rochdale to carry you back to Halifax to end your journey.

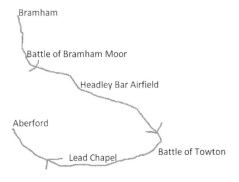

Bus 7 from Leeds will drop you off at the junction of Tenter Hill and Paradise Way on the outskirts of the tiny village of Bramham. Here, you can pause for a moment to get your bearings before setting off in the direction of the first of this walks two ancient battlefields sites. The Approximate distance for this is walk is 7.5 miles.

Tenter Hill is the site of a supposed Roman road and due to its flat open topography, served as a place where "Tenters" were laid out. Tenters were originally large wooden frames which were used as far back as the 14th century in the process of making woollen cloth. After a piece of cloth was woven, it still contained oil from the fleece and some dirt. A craftsman called a fuller cleaned the woollen cloth in a fulling mill, and then had to dry it carefully or the woollen fabric would shrink. To prevent this shrinkage, the fuller would place the wet cloth on a tenter, and leave it to dry outdoors.

The lengths of wet cloth were stretched on the tenter (from Latin tendere, meaning "to stretch") using tenterhooks (hooked nails driven through the wood) all around the perimeter of the frame to which the cloth's edges (selvedges) were fixed, so that as it dried the cloth would retain its shape and size. In some manufacturing areas, entire tenter-fields, larger open spaces full of tenters, were once common and this area was one such place.

The village of Bramham itself stands at the crossroads of the east-west Roman road from York to Ilkley via Tadcaster and the north-south Great North Road, now the A1 road, giving it a history that goes back to the Romans.

The oldest part of All Saints Parish Church in Bramham was built in about 1150 by the Normans. The church consists of nave, aisles, and chancel, with tower and short spire; and has a fine pointed doorway. The churchyard is oval in shape and therefore Anglian in origin.

By 1686, Bramham was a staging post on the London to Edinburgh coaching route and had a population of 291. For many years the village had a rural emphasis, but as the Great North Road grew in importance, the number of coaching inns and stables increased to service the passing trade.

Over the years, a significant amount of employment has been provided by the local estates, particularly Bramham Park and the other grand houses in the village. In the late 20th century there was a decline in employment in agriculture that coincided with the growth of the village as home to a significant number of commuters.

As a result, the village has become increasingly diverse in nature. A large part of the village is included in a conservation area and all the land outside the present built area is currently designated green belt.

After alighting from the bus you head away from the village along Paradise Way towards the sites of two battles from long ago and one of the earliest Aerodromes in the area. Here the land is flat and appears almost endless as it opens up in front of you. As you pass by Bowcliffe Hall on your right this becomes even more evident as the fields do indeed stretch as far as the eye can see. Well as far as Wetherby anyway.

Construction of Bowcliffe Hall commenced in 1805 by William Robinson, a cotton spinner from Manchester. After completing only the West Wing, Robinson sold the property for £2,000 to John Smyth, who finished the estate. Smyth died in 1840 and the house was put into trust by his daughters pending sale. The entrusted estate was purchased by George Lane Fox, whose own house, the neighbouring Bramham Park, had been severely damaged by fire in 1828.

George Lane Fox, known as 'The Gambler', was the MP for Beverley. He died in 1848 and was succeeded by his only son, also George, known as 'The Squire'. The latter died in 1896 and was succeeded by his second son George (his eldest son having become a clergyman) who was MP for Barkston Ash. He renovated Bramham Park and moved back there in 1907. Bowcliffe was then purchased by Walter Geoffrey Jackson, the Managing Director of mining company Henry Briggs Son and Company.

In 1917, the house was bought by the aviation pioneer Robert Blackburn from Kirkstall, the chairman of Blackburn Aircraft Limited who lived there until 1950. He and his family were the last to use the hall as a residential home. As an aviation pioneer, Blackburn built his first monoplane in 1909, making him the first Yorkshire-man to design and produce a powered flying aircraft. Much of his test flying was carried out over Filey, Roundhay Park and Brough. Blackburn made the world's first scheduled flight between Leeds and Bradford in 1914, with the Mayor of Leeds among his first passengers.

In 1955, Blackburn died, and following his death the house was sold to the Hargreaves fuel company in May 1956 for office use, passing into the ownership of the Bayford Group in 1988. Over recent years, Bowcliffe Hall has undergone extensive refurbishment into office space and a corporate and private events venue.

From here Paradise Way runs alongside the A1 for perhaps a mile or so before the junction with Spen Common Lane. It was here that the Battle of Bramham Moor was fought, in the snow, on 19 February 1408. Henry Percy, 1st Earl of Northumberland, who with other nobles had rebelled against King Henry IV, was met here by Sir Thomas Rokeby. The rebels were cut to pieces and Percy was killed, his head, with its silver locks, being carried off and set on a stake on London Bridge.

Percy's army was met by a force of local Yorkshire levies and noble retinues which had been hastily assembled to meet the force, led by the High Sheriff of Yorkshire Sir Thomas Rokeby. The course of the battle itself is not well documented. The action seemingly followed the course of most medieval battles where armies and generals were evenly matched: A violent melee in the centre of the field with little tactical direction.

Percy is said to have positioned his men carefully and awaited Rokeby's arrival at 2.00 pm when battle was instantly joined. It is likely that as with other battles of the era between primarily English and Scottish forces, the outcome was largely decided by English use of the longbow to thin the enemy ranks before charging with their main body. Percy was defeated, and the Earl himself died fighting a furious rearguard action as his army was routed.

In 2008, to commemorate the 600th anniversary of the battle, an information board and a two-sided limestone memorial stone bearing "Bramham" and "Site of Battle" signs were erected on Paradise Way where you now stand. Directly across Paradise Way from this spot is the supposed site of another Roman Road. This whole area is dotted with such roads and MOST of them are totally unknown.

Spen Common Lane itself stretches across the rolling fields towards Headley Hall and your next point of interest. As you stroll along here you may find this type of country lane to be intoxicating and invigorating in the extreme. Flanked by verges, hedgerows, and open arable farmland it should invoke a wonderful pastoral feeling within you. The sky will be open, big and full of light and this along with the land will give you all the freedom you could ever wish for.

Headley Hall and its farm is reached by taking the short track which leads to your right off Spen Common Lane. Make your way towards the huge carnivorous hanger like building away to your right. This whole area is flat in the extreme and it is no surprise it was used as an early aerodrome by The Royal Flying Corps and this building is the only remaining evidence of its prior purpose.

Although nearly a century old the hanger emits something of a modern appearance. Standing close to the entrance is a small unmanned weather station, and as you approach the hanger it is easy to appreciate just why this area was chosen to fly primitive aeroplanes from.

The aerodrome at Headley Bar opened on 18 March 1916 and was set in 198 acres of land of which forty acres were occupied by station buildings. Initially, "B" and "C" flights of 33 Squadron of the Royal Flying Corps were based at the new aerodrome with "A" flight detached to nearby York Racecourse. Following a bombing raid on York on 2 May 1916 by Zeppelin airships, the airfield on York racecourse was closed, and 33 Squadron at RFC Bramham Moor became responsible for the air defence of Leeds, Sheffield, and York against further Zeppelin attack.

Thirty-three Squadron's aircraft were the RAF BE 2c and BE 2d biplanes, these later being replaced by the much better FE 2b biplane. In early 1918, after the RAF was formed, RFC Bramham Moor became known as RAF Tadcaster.

In July 1918, a group of American pilots and ground staff were based at Bramham Moor for training. When the USA had entered the First World War in 1917, their pilots had gone straight into action with a lack of combat experience and had suffered heavy losses. It was subsequently decided that all American pilots should pass through the British training schools such as the one at Bramham.

Within the four years of its existence, the aerodrome saw many changes, with a variety of squadrons moving in and out, as the use of aircraft in WWI developed. During this period, the site was expanded and six 1916 pattern aircraft hangers built, four to the north of the landing ground to the east of Headley Hall and two more at the western extremity of the field. The headquarters for the aerodrome was sited at Headley Bar nearby. The stated complement for the aerodrome was 51 permanent staff officers, 47 NCO above the rank of corporal, 25 corporals, 320 rank and file, a forewoman and 155 women plus 54 (household) women.

The facilities were extensive and included wood, metalworking, sailmaking, doping, machine, smith's and coppersmith's workshops plus storage facilities for ammunition, fuel, and oil. After the Great War, with a reduced perceived need of warplanes, the aerodrome was run down until it closed in the second half of 1919.

It was used for the storage of aircraft for a short period but, after questions had been raised in Parliament, it was decided that the site would not be retained by the RAF. It was then handed over to the Disposal Board and most of the buildings dismantled. It was finally relinquished in March 1920.

Upon leaving this point you walk across the fields for 500 yards before crossing the A64. It may take a while to wait for a gap in the fast-moving traffic and you must proceed with caution. Once you have crossed you are now back in the realms of open fields and deserted country lanes as you travel towards the second battlefield site on this walk.

As you stride away from the busy dual carriageway you will be treated to the fine sight of endless Rapeseed fields on your right and vast ploughed pastures to your left. Hedgerows snake through the fields to signify the ancient boundaries that still hold sway even today. You are now on land belonging to Hazelwood Castle and this whole area overlooks the land on which the Battle of Towton was fought in 1461.

It is from here that you need to be on the lookout for a small beck, and not just any old beck but one that "ran crimson with blood" over five hundred years ago.

This whole area was teeming with men on the 29th March 1461, either arriving at the battlefield or fleeing for their lives from the bloody carnage. In the aftermath of the battle remnants of the Lancastrian forces fleeing the victorious Yorkists were forced to try to cross Cock Beck, having already disposed of most of their arms. Soon the survivors were reported to be crossing the Beck on bridges of their fallen comrades, men struggling across the river were dragged down by currents and drowned. The ensuing massacre of the Parliamentarians is said to have been of such magnitude that the beck ran crimson with blood.

The Battle of Towton was fought during The Wars of the Roses and is described as "probably the largest and bloodiest battle ever fought on English soil". According to chroniclers, more than 50,000 soldiers from the Houses of York and Lancaster fought for hours amidst a snowstorm on that day, which was Palm Sunday. A newsletter circulated a week after the battle reported that 28,000 died on the battlefield.

It brought about a change of monarchs in England, with the victor, the Yorkist Edward, Duke of York—who became King Edward IV (1461–1483) having displaced the Lancastrian King Henry VI (1422–1461) as king, and thus drove the head of the Lancastrians and his key supporters out of the country. The armies gathered at Towton were among the largest at the time. An analysis of skeletons found in a mass grave in 1996 showed that the soldiers came from all walks of life at that time; they were on average thirty years old, and several were veterans of previous engagements. Many knights and noblemen, approximately three-quarters of the English peers at that time, fought in the battle. Eight of them were sworn to the Yorkist cause whereas the Lancastrians had at least nineteen.

The battle took place on a plateau between the villages of Saxton (to the south) and Towton (to the north). The region was agricultural land, with plenty of wide open areas and small roads on which to manoeuvre the armies. Two roads ran through the area: the Old London Road, which connected Towton to the English capital, and a direct road between Saxton and Towton. The steeply banked Cock Beck flowed in an S-shaped course around the plateau from the north to west.

The plateau itself was bisected by the Towton Dale, which ran from the west and extended into the North Acres in the east. Woodlands were scattered along the beck; Renshaw Woods lined the river on the north-western side of the plateau, and south of Towton Dale, Castle Hill Wood grew on the west side of the plateau at a bend in the beck. The area to the north-east of this forest would be known as Bloody Meadow after the battle.

The Yorkists appeared as the Lancastrians finished deployment. Line after line of soldiers crested the southern ridge of the dale and formed up in ranks opposite their enemies as snow began to fall. The opening move of the battle was made by the Yorkists who upon noticing the direction and strength of the wind, ordered their archers to step forward and unleash a volley of their arrows from what would be the standard maximum range of their longbows.

With the wind behind them, the Yorkist missiles travelled farther than usual, plunging deep into the masses of soldiers on the hill slope. Many of the shafts bore bodkin arrowheads, capable of piercing plate armour and penetrating into the flesh underneath. Bodkin arrows were among the missiles that killed many in the battle.

The response from the Lancastrian archers was ineffective as the heavy wind blew snow in their faces. They found it difficult to judge the range and pick out their targets and their arrows fell short of the Yorkist ranks. Unable to observe their results, the Lancastrians shot until they had used up most of their arrows, leaving a thick, prickly carpet of arrows in the ground in front of the Yorkists.

After the Lancastrians had ceased shooting their arrows, the Yorkists archers were ordered to step forward again to shoot. When they had exhausted their ammunition, they plucked arrows off the ground in front of them—arrows shot by their foes—and continued shooting.

Coming under attack without any effective response of its own, the Lancastrian army moved from its position to engage the Yorkists in close combat. Seeing the advancing mass of men, the Yorkist archers shot a few more volleys before retreating behind their ranks of men-at-arms, leaving thousands of arrows in the ground to hinder the Lancastrian attack. As the Yorkists reformed their ranks to receive the Lancastrian charge, their left flank came under attack by the horsemen from Castle Hill Wood.

The Yorkist left wing fell into disarray and several men started to flee. Edward had to take command of the left wing to save the situation. By engaging in the fight and encouraging his followers, his example inspired many to stand their ground. The armies clashed and archers shot into the mass of men at short range. The Lancastrians continuously threw fresh men into the fray and gradually the numerically inferior Yorkist army was forced to give ground and retreat up the southern ridge.

The fighting continued for three hours, according to research by English Heritage, a government body in charge of the conservation of historic sites. It was indecisive until the arrival of the Yorkists re-enforcements. Marching up the Old London Road they hidden from view until they crested the ridge and attacked the Lancastrian left flank. The Lancastrians continued to give fight but the advantage had shifted to the Yorkists. By the end of the day, the Lancastrian line had broken up, as small groups of men began fleeing for their lives.

The weary Lancastrians flung off their helmets and armour to run faster. Without such protection, they were much more vulnerable to the attacks of the Yorkists. Fleeing across what would later become known as Bloody Meadow, many Lancastrians were cut down from behind or were slain after they had surrendered.

Before the battle, both sides had issued the order to give no quarter and the Yorkists were in no mood to spare anyone after the long, gruelling fight. The Lancastrians lost more in their rout from the battlefield. Men struggling across the river were dragged down by currents and drowned. Those floundering were stepped on and pushed under the water by their comrades behind them as they rushed to get away from the Yorkists. As the Lancastrians struggled across the river, Yorkist archers rode to high vantage points and shot arrows at them. The dead began to pile up and the chronicles state that the Lancastrians eventually fled across these "bridges" of bodies.

The chase continued northwards across the River Wharfe, which was larger than Cock Beck. A bridge over the river collapsed under the flood of men and many drowned trying to cross. Those who hid in Tadcaster and York were hunted down and killed as they mayhem and quest for revenge continued.

Here you should look for Cock Beck which is close to a small plantation named Hayton Wood and follow it until you reach the main road. The beck is obviously not stained with blood any longer but it is deep in places so once again proceed with caution. Like the endless stream it is, it winds its way through the battlefield towards the River Wharfe just as it did on Palm Sunday 1461.

Keeping the main road to your left, you now round a bend in the beck and come face to face with the smallest and most humble church you could imagine. This tiny one-roomed building stands alone in the centre of a sheep-filled field. Depending on the season the sheep may graze contentedly right up to the church walls which in itself gives it something of a pastoral setting.

St Mary's Church of Lead is a redundant Anglican chapel standing in an isolated position in fields some 0.75 miles to the west of the village of Saxton. Though technically a chapel, it is generally referred to as a church. Since being rescued by a group of walkers in 1931, the church of St Mary's. Lead has been known as the Ramblers' Church. The repairs made then are recorded on the back of the church door.

The field where the church stands is filled with the bumps and furrows of earthworks that indicate the site of a Medieval manor house, for which St Mary's was probably originally the chapel. St Mary's is a peaceful place and the tiny rectangular building is very simple. It was probably built by the Tyas family, whose massive grave slabs are set into the floor. Carved with heraldic symbols and inscriptions, and dating from the 13th-century, they are an important and interesting collection. The south doorway is probably 12th century, suggesting a much earlier foundation for the chapel. The simple single-cell building is constructed of limestone rubble beneath a stone slate roof. Later additions were made to the church in the 18th-century, with a rustic pulpit, clerk's pew, reading desk and painted texts.

From the church it is only a few metres before you reach the main road and upon emerging opposite the Crooked Billet public house, proceed along the road to Aberford. This rather deceptive fast-flowing road has no pavement running alongside it so once again you must proceed with extreme caution. In a few minutes you will arrive at the sixth-century entrenchment of the Woodhouse Moor Rein on your right. This raised earth banking formed part of a defensive ring that also contained Becca Banks and South Dyke and today can be walked along in peace and tranquillity.

You walk along his ancient track to find it is flanked on one side by thick hedgerows and the only break is the entrance to a superbly named isolated cottage named Reform Place. A little further on you will arrive at the junction with Stocking Lane and turn along here to walk across more open expansive fields towards the village of Aberford. Immediately after you have passed beneath the Aberford bypass glance to your right and only 120 metres away is the clearly visible hump of earth where once stood the village Windmill.

A few metres further on and you will reach Main Street and here you will have arrived at the end of this particular walk and can rest your weary bones on the small 64 bus which will take you back into Leeds central bus station.

Shipley Circle Via Three Salt Family Victorian Mansions.

Shipley is reached by taking any of the 612, 613, 614 or 676 buses from Bradford Interchange. The approximate distance for this walk is 6.0 miles.

Everyone loves an atmospheric and historic old Victorian house but sadly many of these houses are now long gone and all that remains of some is a collection of moss covered skilfully carved blocks of stone in dense patches of woodland.

Often these magnificent residences from a past age have been well documented in print and in photographs but that is not always the case and all that remains are the building plans. Sometimes even those people with first-hand knowledge of such places have followed the buildings into eternity leaving behind them only hearsay and rumours. The focus of this walk around lower Baildon and Gilstead are three such fine late Victorian houses.

To most people today, the names The Knoll, Ferniehurst, and Milner Field mean very little, but to some they invoke images of Victorian splendour, innovation and even excess. The name Salt is recognisable to most local people though and it is this name that is wound around these three magnificent residences like a Serpent coiled around the staff of Hermes. This walk visits the sites of three of the Salt family's historic Victorian homes which are clustered together on the sunny upland slopes overlooking Saltaire.

You can begin this walk in the centre of Shipley and following a short walk you will find yourself in Saltaire, Sir Titus Salt's masterpiece of Victorian social engineering. This Victorian Model Village and World Heritage site is renowned the world over for its innovation and for the vision and philanthropy of Sir Titus Salt.

Salt built neat stone houses for his workers (much better than the slums of Bradford), wash-houses with tap water, bath-houses, a hospital and an institute for recreation and education, with a library, a reading room, a concert hall, billiard room, science laboratory and a gymnasium. The village had a school for the children of the workers, almshouses, allotments, a park and a boathouse.

Because of this combination of houses, employment, and social services the original town is often seen as an important development in the history of 19th-century urban planning. Today the village has changed little and the relevant authorities have resisted any changes that would detract from the small conurbation that Sir Titus envisaged when he constructed it.

After walking along Saltaire Road for half a mile you turn down Victoria Road past neat rows of Salt's worker's houses. They were indeed termed houses as the more humble cottages that Sir Titus Salt's workers had formally occupied in the inner city area of industrial Bradford were literally a world away.

Passing by the magnificent Victoria Hall and its Wurlitzer theatre pipe organ and then the imposing presence of Salts flagship mill you cross the River Aire by way of an iron footbridge before entering Roberts Park. This bridge was constructed to replace the original bridge that was damaged during World War II by tanks making their way to Baildon Moor for training purposes

Originally named Saltaire Park this space is an integral part of the Saltaire World Heritage site. Set in 14 acres and designed by William Gay it was opened by Sir Titus himself on the 25th July 1871. The development included the widening and deepening of the River Aire for boating and swimming purposes and the construction of a boathouse on the southern bank of the river.

The park is divided by a long broad east-west promenade with east and west shelters at the ends. To the north of the promenade are serpentine paths and flower beds and to the south a cricket ground and an open playing field. In the centre of the park is a semi-circular pavilion designed by architects Lockwood and Mawson which was constructed in 1870.

In 1891, the park was purchased by Sir James Roberts and in 1903 he commissioned a bronze statue of Sir Titus and this was erected by the main promenade. In 1920, Roberts changed the name to Roberts Park as a memorial to his Son Bertram Foster Roberts when he gave the park to Bradford Council.

You leave Roberts Park almost as soon as you enter it, passing by one of the entrance lodges before you in the direction of Thompson Lane which will take you on to the ancient hamlet of Baildon Green. This lodge, again designed by Lockwood and Mawson, is a Grade II listed building.

Walking left along Thompson Lane you skirt past the edge of a small council estate with its maisonettes and low rise blocks of flats. Across the lane is the expanse of Walker Wood and Midgeley Wood. Passing by a lovingly restored farmhouse and adjacent cottages at the junction with Green Lane, you take Green Road and pass an old clay pit to approach the historic hamlet of Baildon Green.

Baildon Green is located on a small south facing shoulder of land elevated above the River Aire. The records of early buildings and the occupations of the earliest inhabitants suggest an economy based upon farming and textiles in the 17th and 18th centuries. The construction of Clough Mill by James Clough in the 19th century led to the expansion of the hamlet to house workers, as did the start of quarrying operations at Baildon Green and Baildon Bank. The larger population led to more facilities being provided including three places of worship along with their related schools.

One of these, the former Methodist Chapel named "The Church on the Green" survives today. A public house named The Cricketers Arms was also constructed in 1899. This was preceded by an earlier public house of the same name that was originally situated across the road. This establishment was also called The Smiling Mule. The licence of this pub was surrendered in 1897 and the building is now a private house.

The settlement of Baildon Green went into decline in the early 20th century with the cessation of local quarrying and the decline of the textile industry. Happily today the hamlet retains much of his original character and obvious charm, and as you pass through the hamlet along Green Road and on past the quaint pond of Crutch Well, you turn off along Bertram Drive and towards the site of the long-gone house known as The Knoll.

The Knoll was built for Charles Stead who was the first non Salt director of Salts Mill. This fairly substantial house was a large Victorian mansion of Gothic design which was built in the late 1850s and early 1860s. It was decorated with crenellations and gargoyles and even possessed a tower. Formal gardens were laid out in the grounds with a carriage drive which led down to two lodges, one of which still survives today.

Situated at the top of a hill it would have enjoyed magnificent views across the valley to Saltaire. There are surviving photographs of the house but today no building plans survive. The land on which it was constructed had belonged to the Ferrand family who sold it to Sir Titus Salt who then sold it to Charles Stead for £3400. Charles Stead was declared bankrupt in the 1890s and the house was then sold to Sir James Roberts for £10,000. When Sir James moved to nearby Milner Field his Son Bertram and his family moved into the Knoll.

Members of the family continued to live in the house until after World War I. In the intervening years the house had various owners until being sold to Baildon Urban District Council for £8950. The Knoll was demolished in 1961 and the present day flats were built on the site in its place.

Although nothing of The Knoll remains today, the carriage drive which runs downhill through Fairbank Wood still remains. This is easily accessible to the side of the flats and you follow it along through the heavily wooded area. The tall thick trees form a canopy which almost blocks out the sun and the resulting lower temperature can make you shiver. Here the air is quiet with only the distant bird calls to break the silence.

Thin tracks of hard packed soil lead off in all directions through the undergrowth. You may find the atmosphere slightly oppressive as the light seems to fade away leaving you with only the ghosts of the past as company.

Roughly half way along the carriage drive a small series of steps lead you up the bank to the site of one of the two estate lodges and here you will find the crumbling moss covered walls of the former lodge. From here you resume walking for only a couple of minutes before arriving at the entrance gates by the second estate lodge. The gates themselves are not original but the gateposts are.

A third stone post attached to the side once contained a small gate for pedestrian access. The two main gates are slightly askew and show signs of great age and here you may turn around to check that no ghosts had followed you down from the fine Victorian house which once sat at the top of the hill.

Now you make your way along Southdown road, past rows of 20th-century contemporary houses onto Cliffe Terrace, and after the junction with Southcliffe Drive you turn along Baildon Wood Court. After walking perhaps fifty yards you turn left along a footpath and begin walking towards the area where Edward Salt's mansion named Ferniehurst used to stand.

As with The Knoll very little remains of this once fine Victorian mansion. Again there are no known photographs or building plans, however, maps of the area do show the basic plan of the house and of the glasshouses and other buildings.

Edward Salt married his first wife Mary Jane Susan Elgood on July 10th 1861 and it seems likely the house was built for her. The Salt family lived at the house until 1893 when upon the restructuring of the family business at Salts Mill they left the area to live in Morecambe. Edward Salt died in 1903 and was buried in the churchyard at Bathampton.

Ferniehurst had twelve bedrooms, a tower and a billiard room with its own separate entrance. There were also outbuildings including a carriage house for six carriages, a separate laundry, a gardener's bothy, three vineries and a mushroom house. The house was surrounded by "pleasure grounds" and this was planted with forest trees, herbaceous and alpine plants plus shrubs and ferns of all descriptions.

The house and its estate were bought by George Camille Waud in 1896. His family owned and ran Britannia Mills in Bradford. His great interests were growing roses and breeding Hackney horses and he built a stud farm here to breed these horses.

In the 1920s Waud started selling off land from the estate and in the late 1930s the house and grounds were sold to a quarrying company. It is said they used stone from the house to build properties on nearby Rockcliffe Avenue. Baildon Council then bought the house in the 1940s and demolished it to create an urban area. Some stonewalling, railings and steps are all that remains of the house today. The lodge was on Baildon Road near the bottom of Rockcliffe Avenue and was only pulled down recently. The sad demise of yet another of the district's fine old Victorian mansions was complete.

You approach the estate grounds from the rear and walk up through slightly less dense woodland than that you had just left towards the only remaining building on the estate. Ferniehurst Farm was in its day known as a "Model Farm". The surrounding fields were packed with cattle to provide meat and dairy products for the tiled fully functional dairy. A piggery contained beasts that were destined for the farm's bacon curing room, and the farm even had poultry and Pigeon houses.

Today the farm is still in working order and as you pass along the carriage drive beside it the earthy aroma of the countryside pervades your twitching nostrils. Walking beneath and alongside a massive towering stone wall you will have reached the site of the former Hackney Horse stud farm.

From here you continue on towards the field that once contained the massive impressive glasshouses for Edward Salt's beloved Orchid collection. Salt had one of the foremost collections of Orchids in the country and his Odontoglossum house was considered a model of perfection.

It is downhill all the way from here as you drop down a steep path into part of the gardens now known as The Dell. This expanse of ground surrounded by trees and bushes contains the remains of some stone walls and steps. If you are agile enough you can clamber up one massive high piece of wall and from here look down into what the official Bradford Council blurb calls "an oppressive atmosphere".

Strangely enough, you may find it to be much the opposite as the trees stand around the open ground to form an almost inpenetrative wall to keep the history safe within.

From this point you make your way down the short distance to the main entrance gate of the estate on Baildon Road. The gates came from Baildon Town Hall and are not the original Ferniehurst gates. After a short stroll down Baildon road, we came to the end of Rockcliffe Avenue and the short track named Wauds Gates. This was the original location of the entrance and carriage drive to the Ferniehurst estate.

Here you continue to walk down Baildon Road and after passing the site of the demolished Lower Holme Mills, walk along Otley Road to the junction with Green Lane. The site of Lower Holme Mills was owned for a period in the 19th century by Sir Titus Salt and it is reputed to have been the site originally intended for Salts Mill. This was of course constructed further west along the valley at Saltaire instead. Salt sold the site to C.F Taylor in 1862 who constructed a Mohair spinning and weaving mill on the land.

As is evident so far the Salt family and Sir Titus, in particular, have their footprints all over the area in which you have thus far been walking and the road that you are now heading for is no different. During the 1860's Sir Titus Salt bought up huge tracts of land on the north side of the River Aire, but apart from creating Roberts Park and laying down Coach Road he did little else with it. Coach Road would lead to his Son Edward's house Ferniehurst in the east and the house of one of his other Sons Titus Jnr at Milner Field to the west.

The inheritors of Salts Mill still owned this land after World War II and in 1952 Shipley Urban District Council bought the land and built the present day social housing to replace slums in Shipley, Windhill, and other areas. Shipley Urban District Council's commitment was to blend their housing plans in with the natural environment by consciously resisting the "stack them high pack them cheap" thinking that was common in much council planning in the 1950s.

Some of the residents who moved into their social housing in the 1950s are still living there today as they have never wanted to leave this well-designed estate. The houses on Coach Road and Higher Coach Road were constructed by a multi-skilled labour force put together by the Council named The Shipley Direct Labour Force in the years between 1956 and 1962. According to records, the total building costs for the whole estate were £386,515.

Carrying on along Higher Coach Road you soon arrive at the tiny hamlet of Trench. Surrounded on your right by the ancient Trench Wood this small 17th-century settlement was originally owned by Yeoman Clothiers of the Hudson family with the first record of inhibition being 1665. Trench House can be seen nestled nearby. It is a listed building which has a date stone initialled I H E 1697. This refers to an extension to the house, probably added by Jonathan Hudson who lived there until the 1720s. It is an excellent example of a Yeoman's house.

The front facade of the house is interesting as the builder deliberately moved away from the normal local style and incorporated classical elements. Close to the house is a listed barn, which used to have a date stone of 1669 with the initials SH over a door. Trench Wood itself is a dense semi-natural woodland with Beech and Holly being just two of the wide varieties of native trees and bushes to be found there. Here you turn off Higher Coach Road to follow a small well-worn footpath across Trench Meadow to enter Trench Wood itself.

Once again the wood is rather gloomy due to the densely packed trees and after passing a number of massive Gritstone rocks that may well have been deposited there by an Ice age glacier you reach a marvellously serene and remote millpond. This was the pond and dam for the dye house at Salts Mill and was created in 1911.

Old postcards show this area as Crag Hebble. In the Victorian and Edwardian eras this and the nearby Shipley Glen was a very popular picnic area for the millworkers of Shipley and Bradford. Here, close to the pond in the lower part of the wood, is the remains of Sam Wilson's Toboggan Run which was one of the many attractions associated with Shipley Glen in late Victorian times.

The riders were carried in small cars from the top of the edge of Brackenhall Green down to this area. On Whit Sunday 1900, one of the cars on the upward side fouled the steel cable which lifted it back up to the top. This resulted in several injuries and Sam Wilson immediately closed it, never to reopen it. So ended 'The Largest, Wildest and Steepest Toboggan Slide Ever Erected in the World'.

Also in this area you will see what is known locally as the Bird Cage. This is an elaborate "Kissing Gate" built in 1872 as part of the development of Milner Field house and estate.

A short distance further on you take a track that is known as Sparable Lane. Follow this for a while through Delph Wood and across Little Beck until it turns northwards to skirt alongside what was once the Glasshouse and kitchen garden area of Titus Salt Junior's lavish Victorian mansion of Milner Field.

Walled kitchen gardens were found in many of Britain's large country houses of the period and those of Milner Field were innovative and lavish in the extreme. The kitchen gardens were laid out in well-arranged plots to provide all manner of vegetables for consumption by the residents of the nearby house. In front of the walled garden, there were ten greenhouses, thirty-four feet long and eighteen feet wide. Laying north to south to take full advantage of the sun it was all well planned by the leading Horticulturalists of the day.

Potting sheds were located at the end of each Greenhouse, each being fitted with its own water cistern. Apple and Pear trees grew all around the area to provide fruit for Milner Field's inhabitants. Pineapples were also cultivated here and these exotic fruits were unknown to all but the most affluent of the landed gentry and royalty at this time. A Mushroom house was built near to the boilers. These were sown on soil heaped over damp horse manure.

Now you continue to walk down the path towards the trees where you will enter the site of the long-gone but not forgotten magnificent house of Milner Field.

The house of Milner Field was built on the site of an Elizabethan mansion bearing the same name that Sir Titus Salt had bought in 1869 for £21000 from one Admiral Dunscombe. He immediately demolished the house and passed ownership of the land to his youngest son, Titus Salt Junior, who proceeded to commission the building of a new house. The original Elizabethan Milner Field house was built by John Oldfield in 1603 and Salt Jnr retained the commemorative stone bearing this date and the monograms of Oldfield and his wife and incorporated them in his new mansion.

The grand new version of the Milner Field house was constructed on the sunny northern bank of the River Aire about one mile from Saltaire (but well-hidden amongst trees and gardens), and was amongst the grandest and lavish of any Victorian mansions of its time. When first built it was a wonder of contemporary Victorian living. Sadly, little remains today except for an archive of wonderful photographs of both the interior and exterior, which give a fascinating insight into the lifestyle of well-to-do Victorians such as the Salts.

Work began in 1869 to the plans of the architect Thomas Harris in the (then fashionable) neo-Gothic style, with a nod in the direction of the Arts and Crafts movement. The material used in the construction was "the grey local stone, the outer walls being lined with brick so as to form hollow walls and thereby prevent the possibility of dampness" The roofs were covered with Whitland Abbey green slates bought and transported from Wales.

After leaving Saltaire via what is now Victoria Road and originally crossing a stone bridge, Milner Field could be reached by a carriage drive along a private road westward below Shipley Glen, past Trench Farm and Fell Wood, before reaching South Lodge.

This lodge (also known as Bottom Lodge) was the start of an uphill climb to Milner Field using a long tree-lined approach road through thick woodland. To the left of this road lay a small lake and fishpond with an island and rustic wooden bridge, a boathouse and several rowing boats. Eventually, the road turned left to approach the entrance-way to the house. Milner Field was built facing almost due north and south, the entrance being on the north (rear) side of the building through an arched gateway into a spacious enclosed courtyard.

To catch the sun, the principal rooms of the house faced south and opened onto a wide terrace with steps leading down to the park. Milner Field had its own water and electricity supplies, sewage system and filter beds, water-cooled storage rooms (the forerunner of refrigerators) and was connected by telephone to the mill in Saltaire. It had splendid facilities to cater for the family's recreational needs - a huge billiard room with pre-Raphaelite stained glass and murals, a magnificent library, a music room with a massive purpose-built pipe organ, and stables with buildings to accommodate horse-drawn carriages. It also had landscaped gardens and a large 'winter garden' conservatory connected to the main house via an Orangery.

The Salts entertained lavishly using the nine bedrooms to accommodate their guests and were even visited on two occasions by royalty during their time at Milner Field. Titus Salt Jnr died prematurely of heart disease in the Billiard room on the afternoon of Saturday 19th November 1887. After the death of Titus Salt Jnr, Catherine his wife and George, one of his sons continued to live at the house until 1903.

However in the intervening period and partly because of a trade slump, Catherine Salt was forced to sell the business to a syndicate of four Bradford businessmen. This including James Roberts who within nine months became the Managing Director of Salts Mill. Roberts moved into Milner Field in 1903. He and the next two residents of the house, Ernest Gates and A.R (Teddy) Hollins (a later Managing Director of Salts Co who died unexpectedly in 1929) all suffered a series of personal tragedies. This led many people to believe that the house was jinxed.

The house was put up for sale in 1930, but given the series of tragic events affecting all the owners and tenants, it is not surprising that the mansion subsequently failed to sell. Over the years, nature reclaimed the grounds and the building fell into disrepair, was stripped of its contents and then of its roof, and before long the site began to be robbed of its stone. During the Second World War, it was used for grenade practice by the local Home Guard. Whilst the exact date of demolition of the house is not known local legend suggests a date between 1950 and 1959.

When you reach the site of Milner Field you must tread carefully along a small path that runs towards the ruins that now loom up in front of you. Upon passing through what remains of the ivy-covered main entrance arch you can immediately recognise part of one of the stone gateposts from the original house in the undergrowth. If you turn around here you can clearly see the large flat tree-covered area that was once the Croquet lawn.

Large piles of moss and lichen-covered ornately cut stone lay all around a few feet from you. The mosaic tiled floor of the Conservatory still lies away to the side. Make your way there to stand upon the ground where Royalty once drank fine aged Scottish Whiskey and played cards with Salt and his wife. The remains of the Orangery which connected the Conservatory to the main house are immediately evident as is what remains of the walls of the Billiard Room where Titus Salt Jnr breathed his last.

If you so wish you can mount what remains of the wall here to stand upon the top and gaze down upon the very spot where young Salt writhed in agony as his undiagnosed heart disease took him away to meet his maker. If you have a vivid and lucid imagination it will be in overdrive by this point. Did they carry his body through to the house along this passageway? Was it this one over there? Did they carry him out through the French doors in the Conservatory?

Scamper over the ruins towards the area of the kitchens and here you can see the brick-lined walls and archways of the cellars and storerooms. At one time they will have been filled to the brim with bottles of expensive French wine and fine food from every corner of the world. Today they are stuffed full of rubble and old beer cans.

Stumble over the piles of stone and rubble and you will find yourself near to the south-facing front terrace wall close by what was once an area of manicured lawns, small bushes, and trees. Here you could feel a distinct shiver running down your spine, as if someone has just walked over your grave perhaps. But there might not be any wind or breeze to cause such an unearthly feeling.

Maybe, just maybe, the reports of ghostly happenings here at Milner Field did indeed have some substance and were not just the ramblings of local folk with too much beer in their systems.

Upon leaving the ruins of Milner Field you head for Primrose Lane and head towards the canal. After perhaps five hundred metres you turn left down a footpath at the side of a quaint row of 18th-century weaver's cottages, and within a few minutes you will be standing in the bright sunlight on Dowley Gap Bridge watching a canal boat make its slow unrushed way towards Shipley.

Here the towpath is flat and you can rack up the miles back to Saltaire with little trouble. After crossing over Dowley Gap Aqueduct and the swing bridge at Hirst Lock it is but a short walk along the towpath past Salts gargantuan mill at Saltaire before arriving back at Shipley to complete this walk. From there you can catch any number of buses to complete your journey back to Bradford.

To begin this walk you need to catch the bus 590/592 from Halifax which will drop you on Market Street in Hebden Bridge. The approximate distance for this walk is 8.5 miles.

First you need to walk a short distance along Bridge Gate and turn left where this road meets Keighley Road. From here it is something of an uphill slog to begin until you meet the junction with Midgehole Road but this is some way in the distance.

Hebden Bridge is a market town in the Upper Calder Valley. It is eight miles west of Halifax and fourteen miles north-east of Rochdale, at the confluence of the River Calder and the Hebden Water. The town is the largest settlement in the civil parish of Hebden Royd. The original settlement was the hilltop village of Heptonstall. Hebden Bridge (Heptenbryge) started as a settlement where the Halifax to Burnley packhorse route dropped into the valley and crossed the River Hebden where the old bridge (from which it gets its name) stands.

Steep hills with fast-flowing streams and access to major wool markets meant that Hebden Bridge was ideal for water-powered weaving mills and the town developed during the 19th and 20th centuries. At one time Hebden was known as "Trouser Town" because of the large amount of clothing manufacturing.

Drainage of the marshland, which covered much of the Upper Calder Valley before the Industrial Revolution, enabled the construction of the road which runs through the valley. Before it was built, travel was only possible via the ancient packhorse route which ran along the hilltop, dropping into the valleys wherever necessary. The wool trade was served by the Rochdale Canal (running from Sowerby Bridge to Manchester) and the Manchester & Leeds Railway (later the Lancashire & Yorkshire Railway) (running from Leeds to Manchester and Burnley.

During the 1970s and 1980s the town saw an influx of artists, writers, photographers, musicians, alternative practitioners, teachers, Green and New Age activists. This in turn saw a boom in tourism to the area. During the 1990s Hebden Bridge became a dormitory town, due to its proximity to major towns and cities both sides of the Pennines and its excellent rail links to Manchester, Bradford and Leeds.

Almost immediately the road begins to rise uphill as you pass terraces of industrial revolution age workers houses on the left and over and under dwellings on the right. Notice the huge almost endless stone retaining wall at the junction of Bridge Gate and Keighley road. Here space is limited due to the steep valleys and lack of flat land so in the past, this led to the construction of "upstairs-downstairs" houses.

These were houses built in terraces with 4–5 storeys. The upper storeys face uphill while the lower ones face downhill with their back wall against the hillside. The bottom two storeys would be one house while the upper 2–3 storeys would be another. This also led to unusual legal arrangements such as the "flying freehold", where the shared floor/ceiling is wholly owned by the under dwelling.

The road is lined with humble workers cottages on either side as you continue uphill past Nut Clough, Bessy Bridge and Wood End. Opposite Spring Wood Terrace on your right, walk along Midgehole Road towards an area known as Dog Bottom. Hardcastle Crag is clearly signposted here.

The road now narrows considerably as it runs along the shoulder of the valley. A dense, thick wooded area known as Spring Wood lines the road to your right while Hebden Vale opens up to your left. The aroma of wild garlic here is almost overpowering.in the spring.

Pass by the crumbling buildings of the closed Crimsworth Dye Works on your right and the track down to the long-gone Lower Mill to your left. Note the beautifully restored row of workers cottages named Crimsworth Terrace a short distance after on your right. Three hundred yards further along you will arrive at the area known as Horse Bridge and the car park for Hardcastle Crags with the lodge to your left. From here there are any number of paths leading through the woodland but you keep straight ahead and move through the stone entrance posts on the road.

From here the track continues to rise slightly as it threads its way through Foul Scout Wood, past Foul Hill and Shackleton Wood as it makes its way towards Gibson Mill half a mile away. This landscape was nicknamed "Little Switzerland" thanks to its unspoilt woodland, tumbling streams and spectacular waterfalls, and today it remains a popular beauty spot.

Built around 1800, Gibson Mill was one of the first mills of the Industrial Revolution. The mill was driven by a water wheel and produced cotton cloth up until 1890. Lord Holme Mill — to give it its official title — was erected in the early 1800s by Abraham Gibson, a Heptonstall farmer and cotton spinner, of Greenwood Lee.

Following his death in 1790, it was his son, another Abraham, who set in motion the changes which were to transform the family's cottage industry into a much more ambitious concern; a factory was erected in the heart of Hardcastle Crags and manufacturing began in earnest. Gibson Mill was one of the first generation mills of the Industrial Revolution. The Mill was driven by a water wheel inside and produced cotton cloth up until 1890. In 1833, 21 workers were employed in the building, each working an average of 72 hours per week.

The mill has two water turbines, a large and a small one. The larger one was rebuilt from the original Gilkes turbine which used to power the mill from 1927. Water is fed to a large tank of water from the adjoining millpond. The small turbine takes 50 litres a second (half a bath full) All power is stored in the batteries.

If the large turbine is running and there is excess power generated then this is converted into heat and distributed through a sequence of dump heaters situated throughout the mill. The large array of batteries are proudly on display in the exhibition part of the mill.

Walking on for a further five hundred yards and you will come to Hardcastle Crags itself. The mixed woodland at Hardcastle Crags is managed to encourage natural regeneration of native broadleaved species. Fallen trees and standing deadwood are left to provide habitats for invertebrates, birds and bats. This ancient semi-natural woodland is a mixture of native broadleaf trees (including oak, birch and alder) and planted areas of beech and pine. A rich variety of plant life can also be seen, with species such as great woodrush, bilberry, bluebell, wood sorrel and climbing corydalis.

Species-rich hay meadows can be found high on the valley sides, close to the Widdop Road. The meadows are cut in late summer after the plants have flowered, allowing the seed to be collected. Types of Birds and insects commonly found on meadows include the skylark, twite, meadow pipet, and various types of beetle.

Mill ponds from a past industrial age now provide aquatic habitats for invertebrates, fish, amphibians and birds. The fast-flowing streams of Hebden Water and Crimsworth Dean Beck flow through Hardcastle Crags too. Roe Deer are the largest mammals found here and are easily recognised by their characteristic white rumps. The valley is also home to eight species of bat, including pipistrelle, whiskered, Natterer's and noctule.

Herons, dippers and wagtails can often be found by the river. Rarer birds such as the green woodpecker, redstart, grey wagtail, bullfinch, willow warbler, wood warbler and song thrush can also be seen around the site. Many invertebrates are associated with decaying wood, so Hardcastle Crags provides an ideal home for a number of significant species, including fungus beetles, rove beetles, moths and ants. See how many you can find. Lichens and bryophytes (liverworts, mosses and hornworts) thrive in this area because of the high humidity in the deep valleys. There are also numerous fungi, with over 400 species noted by local naturalists.

Approximately five hundred yards past the crag itself the track splits and here you continue along the left-hand spur to make your way slightly downhill towards a beautiful isolated cottage named Over Wood. Continuing along the path the heavy woodland disappears as it gives way to open moorland in front and the valley of Black Dean to the left.

You are now on New Laithe Moor and down in the valley bottom before you is what remains of the stone foundations of a trestle bridge that once carried a narrow-gauge railway across the valley.

The Blake Dean Railway was an approximately 5.5 miles long narrow gauge railway with a gauge of three feet which ran from Heptonstall to the dam construction sites of the Walshaw Dean Reservoirs. The rail track started in Dawson City, a shantytown built by the Navvies near Whitehall Nook in Heptonstall, along a hillside over several wooden bridges before passing the Widdop Gate and crossing the valley on the trestle bridge to the construction sites of the lower, middle and upper dam of the Walshaw Dean Reservoirs.

The 590 feet long and 105 feet high trestle bridge was constructed of pitch pine. Enoch Tempest contracted the architect William Henry Cockcroft and the local carpenter George H. Greenwood to erect the bridge. It was completed on 24 May 1901.

On 22 July 1906 the bridge caught fire probably by the sparks from the funnels of one of the steam locomotives, but this was quickly noted and extinguished. The damage was only £30, and the bridge was used again one day later. The bridge was sold by auction on 22 May 1912 and disassembled in the same year for recycling the wood.

There were fifteen steam locomotives in use, amongst them 'Esau' and 'Baldersdale'. The family-owned haulage company Hopwood dragged all but one of the locomotives by horse teams from Hebden Bridge up to Heptonstall over the steep road, which winds itself over 300 ft height difference via two hairpins. The transport was normally conducted on Saturday afternoons, when as many as sixteen horses were available.

A fatal accident occurred on 5 September 1905, when the engine driver John Leech and the fireman James Taylor derailed with their steam engine 'Baldersdale' underneath the portal crane of the middle dam. When the locomotive tipped onto its side the driver pushed out the fireman into safety but slipped himself, so that he was scalded by the steam emerging from the boiler. He died a few days later from his injuries.

The navvies used surplus tram cars from the horse-drawn tram in Liverpool for getting to and from the construction sites. They had still their blue and green livery and showed indicated the destinations "Lime Street" and "Fazakerley"

If there is one spot where you rest a while and contemplate the achievements of the Navvies who worked on the great Victorian construction projects this is it. The sheer ingenuity and hard graft of these men is beyond comprehension even today with our dams, bridges and moon landings. Apart from the odd steam engine these men did it with their bare hands and one gets a feeling of great privilege when looking upon what remains of their unearthly endeavours. Sitting here on the valley side you can feel their pain.

From this spot you need to turn around and take a small footpath that crosses over the fields behind you towards a small barn named New Laithe. From here you continue along a small track past New Hay and on towards the hamlet of Walshaw. Once through Walshaw you move along Kiln Lane until it turns to the right but here you continue straight on for 0.7 miles across a small section of moorland known as Hamlet.

Upon reaching a small track bare left and walk for no more than 250 yards then turn right along another track and head for Lumb Bridge and the famous waterfall. This waterfall inspired the famous Poet Ted Hughes to write his beautiful poem "Six Young Men". The poem seems to both be a war poem and a poem about the brevity of human life and the inevitability of death.

Hughes was moved by a photograph of six young men who all died within six months of the beginning of WW1 which was taken at the waterfall. Today, a plaque marks the exact spot where the photograph was taken.

From here carry on over the fields towards the main road. This is Haworth Old Road and from here you turn right and walk for a thousand yards until it meets Keighley Road then carry straight on down the valley back towards the settlement of Pecket Well and ultimately back to Hebden Bridge. Here you can catch the bus back to Halifax to complete this walk.

Spacey Houses to Wetherby

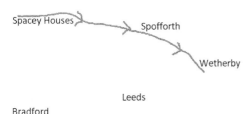

Harrogate

Spacey Houses

Spofforth

Wetherby

Leeds

Bradford

The excellent Flying Tiger airport bus (747) can be boarded at Bradford Interchange and on many points onwards towards Harrogate, and for this walk it will drop you conveniently outside the large BMW garage at the end of Follifoot Road. The approximate distance for this walk is 7.0 miles.

Most walkers love a good railway walk. The old track beds are long and straight with many pieces of interesting infrastructure dotted all around. Many fine Victorian viaducts and bridges remain today and they give a wonderful insight into the skills and naked endeavour of our Victorian forefathers. Many old lines in the West Yorkshire area have now been converted into cycle and walking paths.

It is possible to walk along a good part of the former Church Fenton to Harrogate line between Follifoot and Spofforth and this walk involves doing just that and a little more besides. Harrogate Road is always busy and it may take you a while to cross to the other side to begin the walk up and along Follifoot Ridge. This initial part of the road dissects through Pannal Golf Course as it gently ascends the ridge.

Ignoring the civilised thwacking of golf balls you may wish to glance over to your left to catch the bright sun as it glints off the magnificent distant Crimple Valley Viaduct.

This truly awesome marvel of early Victorian engineering is 1,875 feet long and uses 31 arches, each of a 52-foot span which reaches a maximum height of 110 feet above the Crimple Valley. The viaduct was constructed in rusticated gritstone ashlar and completed in 1848 to designs by George Hudson for the York and North Midland Railway Company. The contractor was the same James Bray that owned and worked the stone quarry at Pool Bank near Otley.

The viaduct was constructed to carry the Harrogate to Church Fenton railway line from Church Fenton to Spofforth which opened on 10 August 1847. The line from Spofforth to Harrogate was completed on 20 July 1848. The Church Fenton to Harrogate line has the dubious honour of being the first line to fall under the infamous Beeching axe with all stations on the line closing in 1964.

The area below the viaduct surrounding the River Crimple (also known as Crimple Beck) gave its name to the synthetic yarn "Crimplene", which was developed at the nearby ICI Laboratory. The fabric enjoyed popularity upon introduction in the 1950s in response to its convenient 'wash-and-wear' properties. Crimplene was often used to make the typical A-line dress of 1960s Fashion. Likewise, it was popular amongst men in British Mod Culture for use in garish button-down shirts.

You will join the old railway line at the end of Prospect Tunnel on the other side of Follifoot Ridge. This badly flooded tunnel runs across the ridge and skirts along the corner of Rudding Park before emerging on Spofforth Moor. Also known by the names Crimple and Prospect Hill, the half-mile long Prospect Tunnel pushed the railway in a straight line under Follifoot Ridge. Three brick-lined ventilation shafts were provided, the deepest being eighty feet. It was down one of these shafts that 24-year-old banksman Ward Dickinson fell 66 feet to his death on Thursday 11th March 1847.

But the tunnel is some way ahead as you continue to climb the gentle slope of Follifoot Range. After passing the small plantation of Spacey Houses Whin on your left you will come to a large and secluded gated property named Alexander House. Its previous name was The Ridge and some time ago two more large houses were constructed in the grounds nearby to the estate lodge on which is now Pannal Road.

A little further on you will pass Beaker Cottages before crossing the road and heading down a tiny track at the side of Prospect House. If it has been raining recently this track through the wooded area could be a veritable morass of cloying mud. Here you will find the entrance to prospect Tunnel which will also be as muddy as a Flanders battlefield. The tiny spec of light at the other end is but a dot twinkling in the distance and only be tempted to venture through if you are equipped with a pair of Fisherman's waders.

The cutting of the former trackbed may only a mile and a half in length but it appears to go on forever due to the copious amounts of sticky mud that may populate its length. Odd sections where the trains wound their merry way through the high, steep and fearsome looking rock faces, line the route. The brooding landscape is broken at intervals by trees that had populated themselves along here since the dastardly cuts of Dr Beeching.

Eventually after fighting through two hundred yards of bushes and slumbering brambles, you will reach Haggs Bridge. Here you have to leave the cutting as the road crosses the trackbed via the partially filled in bridge. After crossing the road you have to negotiate a small but somewhat steep banking to enter the cutting again. The cutting quickly disappears when the trackbed starts to run along a tall embankment.

As you continue to walk along here look down below and through the thin screen of naked trees you will see Spofforth Castle. Here you will arrive at a blocked-off bridge that crosses over a small road below. You must leave the embankment at this point by taking a small path down the side of the bridge to emerge alongside someone's back garden close to a track that leads away to the wonderful and derelict Spofforth Castle.

Spofforth Castle was a fortified manor house, ruined during the English Civil War of 1642–46 and is now a Grade II listed building and scheduled Ancient Monument run by English Heritage as a tourist attraction. Situated on a small rocky outcrop overlooking the village, the ruined structure would have enjoyed a prominent position on the edge of the village. The medieval manor house was arranged around a courtyard but only the West range, which contained the principal apartments still standing.

Only earthworks and some low walls remain of the North, South and East ranges. A flight of steps leads down from the site of the courtyard to the ground floor of the West range. At the South end is the earliest part of the building, dating from the 13th century. The West range was built against the rocky outcrop. A passage cut directly through the rock led up to the great hall but was later blocked, probably in the 15th century.

From the Norman Conquest until the 17th century, Spofforth was in the possession of the Percy family, one of the most important and influential families in Northern England. It was the principal Percy seat until the late 14th century. William de Percy built a manor house here in the 11th century, although nothing remains of this earlier building. Reputedly it was here that rebel barons drew up Magna Carta in 1215. In 1224 Henry III granted a licence to a later William de Percy to hold a Friday market in the town and in 1308 Henry de Percy received a licence to fortify the manor house.

During the Wars of the Roses, the Percys supported the House of Lancaster. Following the battle of Towton in 1461 the victorious Yorkist side, led by the Earl of Warwick, marched on Spofforth, burning the castle and plundering the local countryside. The castle lay in ruins for nearly 100 years until 1559, when it was restored by Henry, Lord Percy. By this time, however, the seat of the Percys had shifted to Alnwick in Northumberland.

The last recorded occupant was the castle steward Sampson Ingleby, who died in 1604. The castle was finally reduced to ruin during the Civil War. In 1924 Charles Henry, Baron Leconfield transferred ownership of the site to the state by deed of gift.

You can enter the ruins through a weather-beaten stone arch to emerge inside the undercroft beneath what would have been the main hall. Probably dating from the first half of the thirteenth century this area of the house uses the rocky outcrop as its fourth wall. The same walls now drip and ooze history out through their stone pores onto the sunlit stone floor below.

Here you can gaze upwards through where the heavy oak floor would have been and into the great hall above. The master fireplace seems to hang precariously fifteen feet up alongside the sidewall. When your imagination is spent you leave the castle area and walk across the small grassy knoll towards Castle Street. In order to continue along the former train line you have to pick it up again on the other side of the village.

So after only a few minutes of walking past quaint centuries-old cottages that line the main road, you reach the turning to East Park Road which leads to the trackbed just before the site of the former station.

The railway came to Spofforth in 1847 with the building of the Harrogate to Church Fenton Line with Spofforth Station being the only intermediate stop between Wetherby York Road station and Harrogate station. The part of the line I was about to join forms the Harland Way cycle path which runs as far as Thorp Arch.

The line continues at the end of East Park Road and before too long the initial canopy of thick trees that lines the trail melts away. The bright sunlight penetrates the now sparse covering of trees to illuminate the former train line and bathe it in radiant light. Wide-open fields stretch away on both sides.

Crimple Beck is still with you at this point, following at a distance before wandering off Northwards towards Ribston with its place being taken by Stockeld Beck. You are now walking along neither a cutting nor an embankment as the trail runs level with the surrounding fields. This part of the former train line is in stark contrast to the part before Spofforth. More bright, airy and warm and because of this the mud will have dried to a firm hardness to make the going easy.

Approaching the area of Malmbury Hill and Kingbarrow Farm you now pass under Ingbarrow Bridge. Stop here for a moment to admire the sooty underside of this simple but highly efficient Victorian bridge. The burnt remains of compressed vegetation from millennia ago coating the surfaces of the stone that had also been hewn from the earth. The cycle of life in a way.

The ancient Market town of Wetherby will now in sight. You have now reached the end of this part of the trail close to Deighton Bridge. Taking a small footpath down through a copse of Sycamore trees you will emerge onto Deighton Road. From here you walk in the direction of the centre of the town to have a look at the thirteenth century Grade II listed bridge that spans the river.

Although the bridge has 13th-century origins it was rebuilt in the 17th century and widened twice, first in 1773 and in 1826 to a design by Bernard Hartley. The bridge was an important logistical link for the coalfields of Garforth and Kippax to the south of the town and settlements north of the Wharfe.

The Artist J. M. W. Turner visited Wetherby in 1816 and painted the bridge, although sadly the vantage point he used is no longer usable owing to tree growth.

You may also notice the ornate antique street lamps that span the bridge on either side. The tiny bus station where you catch the Leeds bound bus is only around the corner so make your way there. The bus travels along the very route and many of the original roads that the 18th century Mail Coach would have done on its steady way back to Leeds bus station to complete this walk.

Dudley Hill to Greengates via Calverley

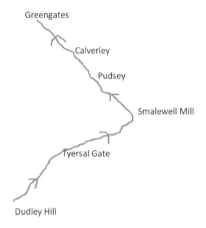

This walk is an easy one as any number of buses bound for Wakefield from Bradford Interchange will take you to the starting point at Dudley Hill roundabout. The approximate distance for this walk is 6.1 miles.

From the roundabout you simply walk a few hundred yards along Sticker Lane to the junction with Cutler Heights Lane. Turn right along here and proceed past the huge Morrison's depot. This somewhat large building stands just where the long gone Greenfield sports stadium once stood.

Today not a trace of Bradford Northern's Rugby Club first home remains but from 1907 to 1969 it hosted not just Rugby League but also Greyhound racing and Speedway. In 1907, the newly formed Bradford Northern rented the ground for £8 from Whitaker's Brewery, who also agreed to sponsor the club. It became Northern's first permanent home and the club set up its headquarters at the adjacent Greenfield Hotel.

Bradford Northern's first match there was against Huddersfield on 7 September 1907 and was watched by around 7,000 spectators. The club gained a significant scalp later that year when they beat the New Zealand touring side.

In 1926, the venue was converted to a greyhound racing stadium, one of the first in the UK, opening in October of that year. By now the facilities were much more developed than they had been in the earlier days. There was a main stand made up of covered terracing on the School Street side, opposite the starting gate. There was also covered terracing along the back straight on the Cutler Heights side. At one end was a huge tote board but no terracing and at the other end, a concourse with betting and a clubhouse overlooking the dog track.

Greyhound racing continued throughout the following decades right up until the stadium's closure. In 1961, a 320-yard Speedway track was laid inside the dog track and the city's speedway team, Bradford Panthers, relocated to Greenfield from Odsal Stadium. The first meeting was opened by the famous speedway promoter, Johnnie Hoskins. Success was short lived and the last meeting at Greenfield Stadium was a double header against Sheffield and Leicester on Tuesday 9 October 1962. The Panthers folded soon after. The stadium was closed for business in March 1969 and was sold for industrial warehousing. The last sporting event was a greyhound meeting on 5 March, attended by 4,790.

From here Cutler Heights Lane leads all the way along to Thornbury roundabout but you do not go that far as you turn off into the countryside at the junction with Tyersal Lane. Cutler Heights Lane itself is flanked with a mixture of modern houses, old grimy cottages and the odd fish shop here and there.

The old train line from Dudley Hill Station once ran parallel to Cutler Heights Lane and the trackbed can still be walked along in places. Just after you turn onto Tyersal Lane you cross an old iron bridge that once straddled the line. It was one of that kind of bridges that no one ever gives any attention to but the huge iron rivets still bare the marks of the foundry that cast them over at nearby Low Moor. Bridges like this one and parts of the general infrastructure of Bradford's long gone rail system still remain today all over the area. People simply pass them by and never give a moment's thought to the skill and ingenuity of the fine men that created them.

Carrying on Tyersal Lane you now head for Tyersal Gate and even though you are walking alongside the edge of what was once the largest council estate in Europe, you will feel free due to the large open expanse of fields on one side. At the junction of Tyersal Lane and Ned Lane you keep to the left and continue past Tyersal Mill. The former worker's terrace houses attached to the mill are still occupied and in good shape.

The busy farmstead of Harpers Gate stands slightly away from the lane behind the mill. Over across the fields to the right you can make out the huge dense expanse of Black Carr Woods which dominates the skyline. Carr Beck runs through here to join with Tyersal Beck a little further on.

The lane narrows considerably at this point, the drystone walls hem you in and funnel you towards perhaps one of the finest and most historic houses in the area. The late medieval timber-framed Tyersal Hall was constructed in 1691 of thin coursed hammer-dressed stone with a stone slate roof. The four-room front has six first floor windows and a single-storey porch with double-depth Quoins. All the windows are double- Chamfered mullioned with almost square reveals. A gabled porch with the Tudor-arched doorway and chamfered surround contains a lintel initialled and dated " RT 1691 ". The interior hall is open to the roof with a mid-19th century elaborate Gothic stair with turned balusters and low panelled walls. The hall is flanked by parlours with plaster ceilings and moulded cornice running around the spine beam.

Here you can stand in front of the ornate iron entrance gates and admire the stout thick carved stone posts. From this point a wall runs around the grounds and this wall is dotted at irregular intervals by strange carvings that jut out from the wall. The thick trees inside the grounds hide the building from prying eyes. The sign warning of CCTV coverage tells you this is not a place to intrude upon and with that notion in mind you must walk briskly down the lane towards the dismantled railway bridges at Black Hey farm.

To your left runs the trackbed of the former Pudsey and Low Moor railway whilst to your right Black Carr Woods encroaches over the fields towards you and the boney woodland finger of Stubbs Rein points across to meet you at the edge of the lane. Now heavily wooded the former train line runs across the top of a huge embankment which once carried it from Tyersal Junction over Tyersal Beck through to Greenside Station in Pudsey.

Here it is not difficult to imagine the dark metallic beasts laden with coal spewing out vast clouds of steam as they roared across the embankment towards the dismantled bridge further down the lane. Here you continue along the narrow lane heading for the farmhouse and barn of Black Hey Farm.

A little further down the lane the huge abutments of the dismantled railway bridge stand proudly on either side of the lane. Here the stonework is untainted by the passing years since its construction and it ushers you along down through the woods towards the ancient stone Clapper bridge that fords Tyersal Beck.

A clapper bridge is an ancient form of bridge which is formed by large flat slabs of stone, often granite or schist, supported on stone piers (across rivers), or resting on the banks of streams. The word 'clapper' derives ultimately from an Anglo-Saxon word, cleaca, meaning 'bridging the stepping stones'.

From here the lane climbs steeply up towards the former busy little area of Smalewell Mill. To the east of Gibraltar Mill, this woollen mill was first constructed in 1821, but on the night of 9th November 1867, a fire broke out in the boiler house. Despite the attendance of Pudsey's brand new fire engine which was successful in extinguishing the fire, the roof fell in and £500 worth of damage was sustained.

Turning left off the lane at this point, you walk along a track through the woods. The wood is lightly packed with trees which allows the light to penetrate down to the rich undergrowth flanking the track. Continue along this path to pass small overgrown delphs on your right before passing the site of the wonderfully named long gone old cottage of Buffy Lump.

After a short while you will emerge onto Waterloo Road. Continue along here for perhaps a mile before arriving at the bottom of Woodhall Lane. Walk up Woodhall Lane and before long you will pass by what was once The Woodhall Estate of The Quaker banker Daniel Peckover.

Daniel Peckover resided at `Woodhall` which stood on the opposite side of Woodhall Lane to Woodhall Lake (on your left). The house was built in the latter half of the 18th century by the Gott family who were the owners of the land in this area from 1755. Daniel Peckover seems to have been one of the great and good of Bradford. Was on the town council and various committees, and often donated money to help get public schemes off the ground.

He commissioned the construction of a huge lake on his land mainly to give gainful employment for the unemployed men of the area. By the side of this lake stood Woodhall Grange, a large Victorian villa. By 1901 (and still in 1911) Woodhall Grange was occupied by Cornelius Metcalfe, a retired waterworks contractor, aged 53. His brother Reuben (also retired) and two sisters (living on their own means) were also present. The Grange is now long gone and apart from a few stone steps no trace of it remains today.

Now you walk steadily up Woodhall Lane towards the tiny ancient hamlet of Woodhall Hills. This timeless small conservation area is centred around the small, nucleated settlement of Woodhall Hills Hamlet, which was originally a collection of workers cottages around Old Hall Farmhouse. A small, central village green still survives. The more recent extension to the west of the conservation area repeats this pattern with a small, central grassed area within the courtyard. To the north of the conservation area is the old Ravenscliffe Farm which is now part of Woodhall Hills Golf course.

The character of the conservation area is influenced by the near universal use of sandstone. In the medieval era, there appears to have been a small community in the area. The current village is the probable site of the documented medieval settlement of Wood Hall.

There are several buildings which contain elements which appear to date from the early modern era. The nineteenth and twentieth century have not seen significant change within the conservation area. The expansion of housing and industry seen within much of Leeds has not occurred and the size and layout of buildings are similar to those on the 1848 Ordnance Survey map.

Several farm buildings have been converted into residential dwellings and this domestication has undoubtedly shaped the character and appearance of the village. The largest change has been to the setting of the conservation area. The two nearby golf courses have impacted upon the landscape surrounding the village and the addition of Priesthorpe Road and Woodhall Road have changed the relationship of the village to its surroundings.

From this point you continue along and down Woodhall Lane as it sweeps down the valley side towards Calverley. Fine green meadows and pastureland open up to each side as Calverley presents itself to you with open arms. You skirt along the edge of this ancient and historic village on your way to its equally historic woods.

The name Calverley is of Anglo-Saxon origin. A ley was a clearing in a wood and is widespread in this part of West Yorkshire (e.g. Farnley, Bramley, and Armley). In this case, it translates to 'a clearing in a woodland grazed by calves.' This would suggest woodland has existed here since at least the 7th Century, but there is also documentary evidence to prove that within these woodlands, trees were being felled for timber as early as 1336.

At the junction with the main road through Calverley, you turn left and after only a few hundred yards take a right turn down Wood Lane to enter Calverley woods. This narrow muddy track is uneven with stones set in the mud and is quite difficult to walk on in places till it improves near the small lodge that guards the lane. Once past here the track opens out and the trees fall back a little.

Here the air is deathly silent and the only sound will be the sound of your footsteps. Set slightly away from the track you will see some red-bricked building remains. Not very high but they peek up above the low and thick undergrowth. These are the remains of an old WW2 army camp where a military training camp was constructed and used to train troops for the D-Day landings.

These buildings later became Guy's Fireworks. Here there was a massive explosion at the factory on June 19, 1957. Local people remembered hearing a bang and a small mushroom cloud appearing over Calverley two or three miles away. Three people died and four others were injured. An inquest was told the explosion occurred when a worker had been drilling into rockets and a spark from a steel bit ignited gunpowder stored in the same hut. The factory consisted of 16 huts in the woods which were formerly an Army and European Volunteer workers camp.

The factory which opened in 1953 and employed up to 80 people at peak production periods was closed on December 31, 1957. The three people who died after the explosion were Peter Lunnis, Elsie Thompson, and Mary Conroy.

A few hundred yards past the ruins you join Clara Drive, and turning left you pass a series of massive, gated modern houses, before crossing Calverley Cutting via the road bridge. By now you are only a few hundred yards from the main road where your journey ends and you can catch the bus back into Bradford, Keighley or Leeds to complete this walk.

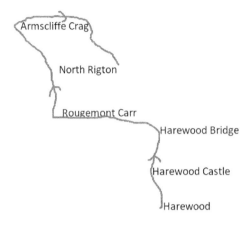

Bus number 36 from Leeds will deposit you almost opposite the Harewood Arms public house to begin this walk. The approximate distance for this walk is 6.5 miles.

From the Harewood Arms it is a slight downhill walk past the historical area known as Bondgate, on past the former site of the village smithy and towards the ruins of Harwood Castle. The trees to your left along this part of the main road are quite thick and you have to be somewhat alert to spot a tiny break in the surrounding wall of the estate. The ruins are clearly visible through the trees and here you must head.

The ruins stand majestic amongst the thickly wooded area but headway can be made from this point. You will approach what remains of Harewood Castle across the former bowling green. Although now studded with tall skinny Larch trees the flat level area gives you a clear indication of its former purpose.

Depending on the time of the day when you visit the area it will be either shrouded in dense cloying mist or bright enlightening sunlight. Either way it is a joy to witness the atmosphere that pervades this area.

The castle was founded by the De Lisle family in the 12th century, and then passed to Sir William de Aldeburgh, following his marriage to Elizabeth de Lisle, heiress of Harewood, who was granted a licence to crenellate in 1366. The rectangular tower house on a steep slope is visible for miles around. The main block of two storeys is flanked by four angle towers, one being a plain entrance tower; the chapel is situated over the portcullis chamber. The lower kitchen wing is of four storeys, with a barrel-vaulted basement containing the well.

When the second Baron Aldeburgh died in 1391 without issue, the castle transferred to the Ryther and the Redmayne (Redman) families, into which his two daughters had married. In 1574, James Ryther and partner William Plompton bought out the Redman family, although Ryther's financial situation must have worsened because he died in London's Fleet Prison in 1595. His son and two daughters sold the castle to Sir William Wentworth of Gawthorpe Hall in 1600 to clear debts; this is probably when Harewood Castle ceased to be a main residence.

The castle was last occupied in the 1630s, and in 1656 it was put up for sale as an 'upstanding source of stone and timber'. The Wentworths sold Harewood and Gawthorpe to Sir John Cutler, 1st Baronet, by which time the castle had probably already been partly dismantled though Cutler lived there at the end of his life. At Cutler's death in 1693, it passed to his only surviving daughter, Elizabeth, Countess of Radnor and on her death without an heir to Cutler's nephew, unmarried Edmund Boulter MP of Boston and Wimpole Hall then to his nephew John Boulter of Gawthorpe and Westminster, who died unmarried in 1738. His executors sold to Henry Lascelles (1690–1753) whose son, Edwin Lascelles, 1st Baron Harewood built Harewood House.

Centuries after it had been abandoned, Harewood Castle remained a landmark and the subject of several paintings in 1797 by J. M. W. Turner. Recent times saw decay and weathering take their toll, and the unstable castle was placed on the Buildings at Risk Register by English Heritage. Then, around the year 2000, a £1 million rescue plan was drawn up, funded partly through English Heritage and partly by the Harewood Estate.

As of 2008, the restoration project, which involved architects, geologists, structural engineers, ecologists and staff of the Harewood Estate, Historic Property Restoration Ltd and English Heritage, was nearing completion. The castle was taken off the Buildings at Risk Register in that year.

On the far side of the castle ruins there is a footpath that will lead you back onto the main road and on towards Harewood Bridge. This historic stone bridge crosses over the river Wharfe and was built circa 1729 by John Carr who was Surveyor of Bridges from 1761 to 1772. Finished in finely-dressed stone, the four segmental arches are separated by three sharply-pointed cutwaters with angled caps.

After crossing the old stone bridge you reach the cottage which was once a public house named The Ship Inn. Then after only a few metres walking you turn left along a small footpath that runs behind the cottage and across the fields. Looking left across the fast-flowing river you may notice the small island that was once the site of Harewood Mill. The white water flowing across the old mill weir bubbles and foams like Beelzebub in a bad mood and confirms that the mill must have been a sizable enterprise in its heyday.

From here the path snakes closer to the river and leads you towards a long stretch of trees that line the bank. Right in the middle of these old trees you will observe the remains of a sluice gate. The iron winding gear is still in place but is seized solid by decades of neglect. Pausing here to catch your breath you will notice the trees of Rougemont Carr about half a mile in the distance. This area of trees and thick undergrowth has, over the centuries, grown up around the site of the mythical and mysterious Rougemont Castle. As you approach the edge of Rougemont Carr you must be aware that the site of Rougemont Castle is a protected area, but as long as you stay on the footpath things will be ok.

Rougemont Castle was an early medieval earth and timber ringwork fortress, founded by the de Lisle family. The ringwork now stands on a steep north bank, where the River Wharfe turns a right-angle at the confluence with Weeton Beck. Most of an inner platform is missing, undermined by the river but a rough D-shaped ringwork with a raised interior remains. Encased by a wide ditch and an inner bank, visible masonry in the bank indicates the remains of a wall.

The ringwork lies on the south-east corner of a larger D-shaped enclosure, encased by a wide bank and ditch, with the Weeton Beck and the River Wharfe to the south. The western gap in the bank is probably the original entrance and along the beck is the remains of a group of fishponds.

A bank one metre high and three metres wide follows the inside of the ditch and masonry visible in places indicates the remains of the stone wall that crowned the ringwork during the Middle Ages. At this time the site was the centre of the manor of Harewood and, as such, the ringwork would have contained important domestic buildings including the residence of the Lord of the Manor. The ringwork lies towards the south-east corner of a much larger D-shaped enclosure formed on three sides by a bank and infilled external ditch measuring one metre high by three metres wide and three metres wide respectively.

The southern side of the enclosure is formed by Weeton Beck and the Wharfe. This enclosure formed the bailey of the castle and would have contained ancillary and garrison buildings and pens for corralling stock and horses. Now woodland, the manorial site was abandoned in 1366 when Harewood Castle was built.

Stand in the centre of this sizeable copse of thin trees and try to make some sense of this ancient place. Due to its age, this early medieval earth and timber ringwork fortress is not something you will come across every day, but one thing you will see is exactly why the structure was built in this location. Here the river is strong and would have formed a perfect defensive line on one side.

Here, if you are lucky, you may be fortunate enough to see a young Fawn Deer shoot out from behind a hedge, run a few metres then stop deadly still. She will be so close you can clearly see the myriad of white spots on her silky flank. The whole scene may only last a couple of seconds but it will feel like two years, before with a flash the Deer will be gone.

After clearing the woods, the ancient footpath continues through Rougemont Carr before meandering across a meadow towards Weeton Beck. It is at this point that the beck is crossed by a fantastic tiny Packhorse Bridge.

A packhorse bridge is a bridge intended to carry packhorses (horses loaded with side bags or panniers) across a river or stream. Typically a packhorse bridge consists of one or more narrow (one horse wide) masonry arches and has low parapets so as not to interfere with the horse's panniers. Packhorse bridges were often built on the trade routes (often called packhorse routes) that formed major transport arteries across Europe and Great Britain until the coming of the turnpike roads and canals in the eighteenth century.

From here the footpath joins a more substantial track which winds its way past a sewerage depot and along to Gallogate Lane and onto Weeton village. This lane takes you to within touching distance of St. Barnabas's Church, its Vicarage and Weeton House. From here you head towards Weeton Lane and beyond that the former estate of The Limes.

Today a peaceful little Cricket ground stands on part of The Limes's estate. It is home to Weeton and Huby Cricket Club. The simple changing rooms and scorebox appear to have seen better days and the gated entrance to the former estate still stands and is used by players to access the cricket pitch.

After crossing underneath the railway line via Weeton Bridge you will soon be on the extremely busy Harrogate Road. Stay on this side of the road until you reach the junction of Crag Lane and Woodgate Lane. Here you must cross this busy stretch of road and begin the ascent to Almscliffe Crag.

The Millstone Grit outcrop of Almscliffe Crag is only 0.6 of a mile away but appears to be a lot further. From here it is all uphill so you must dig those heels in to propel you towards its weatherbeaten summit.

After one hundred and fifty yards you turn right up Holly Hill towards Hollyhill Farm. At the side of Hollyhill Farm take the small footpath that will take you over the rising fields. Here the vista is incredible and it appears that the whole of Wharfedale is spreading itself out before you for your inspection.

It compels you to see it, feel it and walk it. More than that it inspires you to dig deep and finish the climb to Almscliffe Crag because you want an even better view than the one you are now enjoying. The ancient and mystical draw of Almscliffe Crag now pulls you towards it like Egyptians to a Pharaoh's Pyramid.

This footpath terminates as it meets Crag Lane and here you turn left along the road towards the crag. The stile in the wall opposite Crag Farm funnels you over and into the field and from there the path leads you between twin stone walls and up towards the ancient and mystical Crag.

Almscliffe Crag is a Millstone Grit outcrop at the top of a small hill near the village of North Rigton. The crag was formed due to the softer adjacent strata of shale and mudstone eroding at a faster rate than the hard-wearing millstone. Connected by folklore to the Cow and Calf rocks on Ilkley Moor, this place is worth a visit if only for the great views and weirdly weathered bowls in the stone. Standing stones reputedly once stood nearby, so it seems very likely that the sacred nature of the crag was recognised by our ancestors.

The Crag is a prominent group of Millstone Grit rocks, said to have been sacred to the religion of the Druids, and still retains many traces of the rites and observances of their faith. One rock is named the Altar Rock, and near to this is a natural opening in the cliff, about eighteen inches wide and five feet in height, which is known as the entrance to the "Fairy parlour". It is said to have been explored to the distance of one hundred yards, and to end in a beautiful room sacred to the "little people", a veritable fairy palace. Other reports say, that it is a subterraneous passage having an exit near Harewood Bridge - some two or three miles distant.

With the exception of the entrance to the fairy parlour, all the openings in the rocks are carefully walled up to prevent foxes from earthing in the dens and caverns within. On the surface of the main group of rocks are several basins or depressions, no doubt formed principally by Nature. An old custom of the local country people was the dropping of a pin into these basins, they believing that good luck would follow this action.

One of the basins is known as the Wart Well; anyone troubled with warts came here and pricked them until the blood flowed freely into the basin, and finished by dipping the hands into the water. If their faith was great enough, the warts were seen no more.

In the year 1776, a young woman of Rigton, having been disappointed by her lover, determined to commit suicide by leaping from the summit of the rocks, a distance of nearly fifty feet. A strong wind blowing from the west inflated her dress, and in her perilous descent, she received very little harm. She never repeated the experiment and lived many years after.

The Crag can clearly be seen from afar, in all directions, as a large knobbly hill. From the top, on a clear day, you can see for over forty miles with Ferrybridge and Drax (near Selby) power stations visible on the horizon. If you wish to climb to the very top of the crag you may wish to make your way around to the rear of the formation. Here there are many easy and short routes onto the top of the rocks and from there it feels like you are standing upon the very roof of Wharfedale.

All the effort you have expended on this walk has led you to this precise spot and this perfect moment in time. Ancient people had witnessed what you are now seeing, and the weather, seasons, animals and landscape will have influenced and shaped their lives to a huge degree.

Ilkley Moor and beyond it the Aire Valley stands like a conduit to another world, the omnipresent Chevin stretches herself out and shows the way. You whirl around like a Dutch Dancing Doll to lap up the 360-degree panorama of the landscape before you. It really is the view to see before you die.

When you have had your fill of one of Mother Natures finest sights you reluctantly make your way down from the outcrop and back towards Crag Lane. You have to catch the hourly 747 Airport bus back to Bradford so you must begin to make your way towards the village of North Rigton.

Punctuated only by the odd quarry, Crag Lane is flanked on either side by open pasture until you reach the splendid eighteenth-century New House close to the village. From here the lane followed a sharp descent past Spout House to the area known as Mawking Hill and on to the main road from where you can catch the bus back to Bradford.

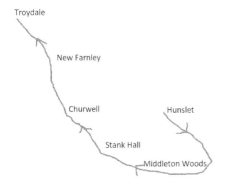

Dewsbury Road in Hunslet is reached by the 74, 110, 189 or 410 bus from Leeds Bus Station. From there you need to walk along Tunstall Road then turn right at the roundabout then walk to the Middleton Heritage Railway Depot. The approximate distance for this walk is 6.4 miles.

This walk is a little different as it begins with a short trip on a steam train. The smell, sound, and vibration of these monstrous machines are intoxicating and not at all geeky. Although some people would disagree with that statement steam engines have to be respected for their historical importance alone. The invention of the steam engine kickstarted the Industrial Revolution and that, in turn, led to the world and society that we enjoy today. Some say this had even greater importance than the advent of the Internet, and although that is open to interpretation there is no doubt that the steam engine changed things massively.

The Middleton Railway is the world's oldest continuously working public railway. It was founded in 1758 and is now a heritage railway, run by volunteers from The Middleton Railway Trust Ltd. since 1960. The railway operates passenger services at weekends and on public holidays over approximately 1 mile of track between its headquarters at Moor Road, Hunslet and Park Halt on the outskirts of Middleton Park. Coal has been worked in the Middleton area since the Thirteenth Century and the railway has its origins in the transportation of this substance to the growing city of Leeds nearby.

The Middleton Railway, the first railway to be granted powers by Act of Parliament, carried coal cheaply from the Middleton pits to Casson Close, Leeds (near Meadow Lane, close to the River Aire) The line was privately financed and operated, initially as a wagonway using horse-drawn wagons. Around 1799 the wooden tracks began to be replaced with superior iron edge rails and the cheap Middleton coal gradually enabled Leeds to become a centre of the many developing industries which used coal as a source of heat, e.g. for pottery, brick and glassmaking, metalworking, and brewing, or as a source of power for mill and factory engines.

In June 1960, the Middleton Railway became the first standard-gauge railway to be taken over and operated by unpaid volunteers. Passenger services were initially operated for only one week, using an ex-Swansea and Mumbles Railway double-deck tram (the largest in Britain seating 106 passengers), hauled by a 1931 diesel locomotive hired from the nearby Hunslet Engine Company. However, the volunteers of the Middleton Railway subsequently operated a freight service from September 1960 until 1983. Regular operation of passenger services began in 1969.

Your destination is Park Halt in Middleton Park. Located close to the site of the former Broom Pit colliery, Park Halt railway station is the current terminus of services at the far end of the line. Branches once continued to Day Hole End and to West Pit via a rope-worked incline. There were also numerous wagonways from early pits in the park, the remains of which can still be seen today. The station consists of a platform for Middleton Park and a run round loop for trains allowing return running.

Middleton Park itself is a remnant of the manorial estate which existed after the Norman Conquest and is mentioned in the Domesday Book of 1086. At the northern end of the park, there is an earthwork from 1204 demarcating the boundary between Middleton and Beeston. Lords of the manor included the Grammarys, Creppings, Leghs, and Brandlings.

The Brandlings cleared land and built Middleton Lodge circa 1760, creating a country estate. The Brandlings exploited the underlying coal and were responsible for building the Middleton Railway to transport the coal into Leeds. The area contains a large number of "shaft mounds" which are thought to mark sites of medieval coal mines. Survey work was done in 2007–2008 to discover more about the mounds, which seem to represent various mining techniques, including Bell pits, cog and rung and Whim Gins.

A whim also called a whim gin or a horse capstan, is a device similar to a windlass used in mining for hauling materials to the surface. It comprises a capstan or a wide drum with a vertical axle. A rope is wound around the drum, with both ends traversing several pulleys and hanging down the mine shaft. As the drum is turned around, one end of the rope is lowered, carrying an empty bucket, while the other one is raised, carrying a full load.

The major benefit of using a whim is that the whim's operation can be performed at a distance from the shaft, thus resolving some of the congestion. Early whims were horse-powered, but later they were powered by waterwheels or steam engines, including the most advanced Cornish engines. Whims were used in coal mines until the end of the nineteenth century.

After leaving the train you walk through the woodland. It imparts a feeling of antiquity with the knarled aged trees seemingly watching every step you make along the tarmac track. This seemingly innocent and unobtrusive track had a massive significance to the local coal mining endeavours of the 1750s and 1760s.

The reason for this is it lies on the route of a wagonway which had wooden rails and was used to transport coal downhill to Middleton railway from where horses would haul the coal trucks into Leeds. Horses would also be used to bring the empty wagons back up the incline to once again be filled.

Although oak dominates the woodland, a variety of other species including birch, hazel, elder, sycamore, beech and sweet chestnut can be found. However, it is not just living trees that are important - old, dying and dead trees, rotting, fallen timber and decomposing leaves all provide food and shelter for a wealth of invertebrates, particularly woodlice, spiders, millipedes, and beetles. These, in turn, are eaten by mammals and birds including bats, mice and voles and woodpeckers and treecreepers.

The remains of previous coal mining activity are evident all around in small spoil heaps that line the trajectory of the tarmac track. Used by local youths as BMX trails these heaps today stand as silent testimony to the skills and sheer hard graft of the Middleton miners.

You exit Middleton wood by South Leeds Golf Course, and cross Beeston Park Ring Road to make your way towards a tiny footpath that will take you to a place named Stank Hall.

Stank Hall is accessed by crossing over the railway via a heavily caged and fenced off bridge. The reason for all the protection is due to the high number of people jumping from the bridge onto the line and trains below. Surrounded by trees and nature the oppressiveness of the steel cage over the bridge is a stark reminder that life is not always good and great in this fairy dairy world we live in.

Standing 500 yards from the White Rose Centre, Stank Hall is reputed to date from 1420 and was allegedly rebuilt in 1492 using some of the timber leftover from the construction of the Christopher Columbus ships, the Santa Maria, Niña and Pinta. The stone building attached to the barn is said to have been used as a chapel by Major Joshua Greathead (1616-1684) who fought in Cromwell's army at the Battle of Adwalton Moor in 1644. At the time Stank Hall Farm belonged to the Royalist John Hodgson. The farmhouse to the right can be dated back to 1615. It is in two parts, one built of stone the other of brick with stone facing.

Christopher Hodgson was one of the earlier owners. The Hodgson family sold it to Thomas Kitchingman who was once a Mayor of Leeds. In 1796 Robert Dennison bought the property, it then passed into the hands of the Scrutton family. It was eventually sold to the Middleton Fire-Clay Company, then Leeds City Council.

Some of the main elements of a timber-framed building survive within the brick walls of Stank Hall. They are probably the remains of the earliest house, perhaps built at the same time as the adjacent timber-framed barn.

The latter has been tree-ring dated to between 1448 and 1490. There are also some masonry remains, including a latrine closet and adjacent fireplace that may date to the 16th century. New Hall, originally a stone wing built on to the south end of the hall, was erected in the 17th century, probably by the Hodgsons.

New Hall was an additional wing to the south end of Stank Hall, probably built in the early 17th century by Christopher Hodgson after he purchased the property in 1609. By the 1950s New Hall was a separate property from Stank Hall Farm and was divided into three houses. The name, Stank Hall is allegedly devised from the number of stagnant pools of water which were in the area.

The building on the left is Stank Hall which was the house associated with Stank Hall Farm. The building on the right is New Hall which was divided into three houses which in 1949 (until the 1990s) were the homes of the Cowell, Wilson, and Slater families. Stank Hall Farm was owned by Sydney Cowell and his family; they continued farming the estate using the manorial barn for storing hay and corn, stabling horses and sheltering cattle until the mid-1960s. There's been patch-ups and partial rebuilds in the 16th and 17th centuries but the core of the building is around 500 years old. Which makes it interesting and important given how little of medieval Leeds survives.

The barn is made of a timber frame resting on a stone sill (to stop the posts rotting) and was covered in thackstones - medieval roof tiles. It was originally clad in wattle and daub which was later replaced with stone. The size of the barn reflects the fact that grain needed to be stored on a large scale in medieval times and was typically held in these protected barns away from the weather and pests.

Leaving behind this wonderful reminder of Leeds's medieval history you descend down the hillside and dodge the fast-moving traffic on Dewsbury Road. Once you have done that you have to move towards the far side of the massive car park of the White Rose Centre and head for the only railway bridge for miles around.

From the viewpoint on the bridge, you can clearly see across the lush green fields to your next destination of Elland Road in the middle distance. Now you must head towards the viaduct that carries the railway line that you have just crossed over Elland Road. Once underneath the viaduct it is only two hundred metres downhill to the site of the Churwell Tram crash.

On the 12th May 1923 Tramcar 191 lost control on Churwell Hill, close to the old Town Hall and crashed near Ingle's Leatherworks on Elland Road. The crash occurred when the tramcar was derailed and hit a wall before overturning. The impact separated the top deck from the lower deck and seven people were killed, with thirty-five others sustaining injuries. Two of the men lost their lives in a brave attempt to stop the tramcar, which was conveying passengers who worked at W.L. Ingle Ltd., leatherworks.

As you stand on the exact crash site and look back up the road, you may wonder how the lumbering trams made it up the steep gradient. In later times it wasn't uncommon for bus drivers to come into the shop asking for water for their boiling radiators when they reached the top bus stop just outside the church. The crash was instrumental in having the tram-car service from Morley down through Churwell discontinued.

From here you head back towards the hill and walk along Old Road on your right before joining New Village Way. Walk along here for a short while until you reach a track that turns off to the right and follow this towards the motorway. Now you take the short tunnel that runs beneath the motorway and upon exiting the tunnel continued along the narrow lane towards the numerous rows of graves that stand silently in the field to your left. in a field.

As you draw closer to the field you can see that most of the headstones are white with the occasional black one mixed in here and there. Each one carries a Star of David sign cut into the granite along with wonderful names such as Ebeneezer, Solomon and Gideon.

The track terminates as it joins Gelderd Road and from here you bare right and continue to walk for one hundred and fifty yards before taking a small cobbled track on your left that climbs up a hillside on the other side of Geldard Road. Here at the top you can see a jumble of cock-eyed old gravestones in the undergrowth to your right. These graves are old and forgotten but have a certain air of gravitas that compels you to stay and rest awhile amongst them.

Here you may wonder who Zephaniah Glass was. He was old when he died but what kind of life had he lived? Was he a pious religious family man of unimpeachable reputation or was he a shady moneylender who made a fortune trading on other people's misfortune?

What had Jedidiah Jotham achieved in his life? Had he been an accountant and a Freemason of fine standing or a pervert like his Father? These and more wonderful names of the long-dead surround you. The gravestones here like the ones further down the hill are simple in design and not at all like the Victorian graveyards that you may have seen before. There are no massive and imposing mausoleums or grand carved headstones like at Undercliffe Cemetery in Bradford for example. These are just simple graves in the undergrowth. They belonged to simple people who were humble Jewish Tailors and the like not leaders of men who built grand mills and made fortunes.

From here you have to move back through the bushes and onto the track. Once again the vast fields reveal themselves before you. Flat and broad to your left towards Gildersome but rolling down in front of you towards Whitehall Road. From this point you can see a tiny patch of trees to the east marked as Farnley Wood on the old maps. From there a small track named Wood Lane will lead you down onto Whitehall Road and ultimately to your final destination of Troydale. Upon joining Whitehall road you turn left and walk on for a short distance until you reach Back Lane also on your right.

The area you are now in is known as New Farney and this did not exist as a village until the early part of the 19th century when Edward Armitage started the Farnley Iron Works and Farnley Fireclay. He needed many workers so he built houses for them, and what had been known as part of Farnley now became New Farnley. Established in 1844 by the Armitage Brothers, of Farnley Hall, to make use of the minerals — coal, iron, and fire-clay — on their estate, operations were confined to the manufacture of pig-iron in cold blast furnaces and production of wrought iron plates, bars, axles, etc.

Now you walk along the tranquil Back Lane following the route of Tong Beck as it passes through nearby Cockersdale. The beck becomes Pudsey Beck a short distance from here on the corner of Troydale Lane as it passes what was known as Farnley Mill. At the junction with Tong Road you turn left and walk for two hundred yards before turning right along Troydale Lane.

Troydale Leather Works is but a short distance ahead and this place also took advantage of the water power provided by the beck but today the site is occupied by a small estate of modern housing.

It was here that your journey ends and you can catch the bus into Pudsey and thence on into either Bradford or Leeds. As you sit in the grass waiting for the bus to Pudsey you may find yourself thinking back to the old Jewish people buried in the overgrown hilltop cemetery.

The heavy snow of Christmas falls and then as the weather improves the hot summer sun bleaches the headstones a little more as one year turns relentlessly into the next. Time marches on and the only changes in that hilltop graveyard are the Blackberry bushes as they live through their cycle of life.

The 425 or 427 bus from Bradford Interchange will drop you outside the Railway public house on Moorside Road right beside the Battle of Adwalton site. The approximate distance for this walk is 4.2 miles.

The pub car park stands on the site of the long-gone Drighlington and Adwalton railway station. This tiny station was opened on the 20th August 1856 and closed on the 30th December 1961. Today nothing remains of the station.

The First English Civil War touched the West Yorkshire area quite substantially. The towns of both Leeds and Bradford were involved in sieges and various skirmishes involving the Royalists and Parliamentarians. The word town is used as both Leeds and Bradford were not cities at this time. But the only battle of note inside the official Bradford area was on 30th June 1643 at Adwalton moor on the edge of Drighlington. In fact, it was the only battle of any age and as such makes a great starting point for this walk.

The site of the battle of Adwalton Moor is on high ground on the edge of the village of Adwalton, now commonly considered to be part of Drighlington. The Earl of Newcastle, the Royalist Commander, was marching on Bradford (which was Parliamentarian in sympathy) with 10,000 men. Fairfax, the Parliamentary commander, had 3,000-4,000 men in Bradford. However, despite his inferior numbers, Fairfax came out to intercept the Royalist army as Bradford was ill-prepared to resist a siege. The battle was of medium-term significance, and victory consolidated the Royalist control of Yorkshire.

The Parliamentarians achieved initial success, but once they were out on the open moor there was a sudden change of fortune. The Royalists' pikemen pushed the Parliamentarians back, their cavalry turning the retreat into flight. The Royalists had won. The victory at Adwalton Moor gave the Royalists control of the North for the remainder of the year. It was second only in significance to Marston Moor in the history of the Civil Wars in the North.

On the battlefield site the landscape of 1643 was one of the hedge-lined fields on the lower slopes and moorland with coal pits higher up. The expansion of housing and roads over the last 150 years has dramatically altered the character of the battlefield.

To begin this walk you need to move the few yards towards the edge of the moor and mount the small ridge that runs almost the whole length of the East side of the battlefield area. From here you can survey the whole battlefield site.

Armed with a vivid imagination it is easy to conjure up a picture of what the day's events during those three hours may have looked like. Although the air is still and silent you can almost hear the scared and excited shouts of the Parliamentarian foot soldiers as they rushed The Royalist lines on the exact spot where you now stand. The smoke from the few cannons available that day swirled all around to envelop the battlefield. The metallic clashing of the steel weapons and nervous whinnying of the horses only added to the confusion.

Thousands of men were fighting for their beliefs, their families, and their very lives. The screams of the injured and the dying filled the air, cursing their King and all he stood for as they met their God. Lead musket balls flew through the confusion before tearing through human flesh and bones, the earth stained with blood and covered with shattered bodies.

Confusion reigned all around as The Royalist Cavalry chased the Parliamentarians from the battlefield in the rout. Scrambling through hedges and falling into ditches they did their best to survive the onslaught but the Cavalry was persistent and hunted them down with no mercy to complete the victory. This now silent patch of open common was once a killing field and it comes alive in front of you.

Today the former battlefield is visited by dog walkers and the odd person with too much time on his hands. But now you have to break the spell as you had to move on because you have a lot to see and a long way to go. So moving through the open moorland you head for Whitehall Road which will take you to the nearby area of Drighlington.

As you pass through the crossroads you will notice up ahead an unusual church spire. The spire has the shape of a square battlement rather than the shape of a normal spire. Upon reaching the churchyard pause here for a few moments to admire the church of St. Paul. Constructed over two years from 1876-78 this Grade II listed building of hammer-dressed stone with a Welsh blue slate roof stands proudly indeed even with its unusual steeple.

A short distance past the church you turn up Back Lane and walk for a short while before arriving at the magnificent Lumb Hall. Originally built in 1640, this Grade I listed house was home to the Yeoman Clothiers of the Brookes family. One of a group of small mansions built in the "Halifax" style in the period between 1630-1660, it is believed to be the only remaining house in the area which dates back to before the nearby Battle of Adwalton.

This fine house of well-coursed gritstone and stone slate roof has many mullioned and transomed windows and coped gables. Above the front porch is a "Wheel Window" familiar to all the houses in the Halifax style. It is also reputed to have a ghost called Charlie who appears in Civil War attire and wanders around the ground floor.

Back Lane leads you to a small public footpath that crosses a golf course and takes you across the valley towards the ancient village of Tong. Dodging the flying golf balls you keep on this footpath and enter a small wooded plantation named Doles Wood before crossing the site of a former tiny Colliery of the same name. This coal pit was operational from 1863 to 1887 then reopened in 1908 for a short time. On the 2nd of March 1865, it was rocked by an explosion that took the lives of three local men.

Now you cross Ringshaw Beck via a small ancient flagstone Clapper footbridge which leads you to a series of open fields. From here the view back across the valley to Drighlington is superb so you may decide to stop for a while and rest. From this point the quaint village of Tong is only a short distance up the valley side so gather yourself together and set off once again.

The footpath takes you up the hillside to emerge alongside the former village school. From here you turn right along the main road and walk for only a few hundred yards until you reach Keeper Lane. Turning up Keeper Lane at the side of what used to be the village Pinfold, you may want to look back over to the small Cricket ground by the side of The Greyhound pub. This is said by many to be the most picturesque Cricket ground anywhere around the Bradford area with its small quaint pavilion. The sound of leather against Willow whilst supping a pint of well-brewed local ale takes some beating.

The Greyhound, a former coaching inn famous for its collection of Toby jugs, replaced the original village pub at number five, Tong Lane, when it was built in 1840. The Pinfold which measures twenty feet square stands next to what was once the village Smithy and Wheelwrights shop. Here you may notice a water hand pump adorned with a Lion head spout.

From here you now walk along Keeper Lane which after a short distance becomes a narrow bridleway closely bounded by drystone walls. This ancient right of way snakes its way down past the grounds of Tong Hall before crossing Pudsey Beck and rising again up towards Bankhouse and Fulneck.

Passing East View Croft with its long barn with two arched entrances you now arrive at The Manor House. This superb Grade II listed residence was originally built in 1629 with an added 17th-century eastern wing which stands behind stout iron gates. Sir George Tempest lived here for a while when his usual residence of Tong hall was being rebuilt. Look out for the most delightful lake standing in front of the house. Situated in mature lawned gardens surrounded by trees that sweep low to kiss the water it looks simply superb and idyllic. Between the house and the lake is a kind of terrace fronted by small stone pillars that also sweep down to the water's edge.

Now continue along Keeper Lane and walk down this heavy tree lined ancient packhorse trail towards the bottom of the valley. As you tramp downwards past centuries old trees, images of simple country folk leading their horses down this very track may come to mind. The saddles and panniers of their Packhorses piled high upon the plodding beasts as they wind their way towards the crossing point of the beck below.

After passing by an old disused quarry on the edge of Acre Wood you come to the point at the bottom of the valley where Pudsey Beck is joined by Holme Beck. Here the trees are sparse allowing the sunlight to bathe this small area. This gives it a peaceful and pastoral feeling that may make you want to stay awhile beside the trickling waters of these age-old becks.

The occasional cobbles are hard on your feet as you climb up the valley side. The trail seems to go on forever and you may have to pull in deep breaths as you plod along. Here, huge exposed tree stumps in the tall surrounding earth banking laugh at you with disdain at your obvious struggle to climb the valley side. But before long you reach Bankhouse and can take a well deserved breather after your long exertions.

Now you are not far from the Moravian settlement of Fulneck. First established in 1744 when Protestants from Moravia came here after fleeing forced Catholicism back home. It is named after Fulneck, the German name of a town in Northern Moravia, Czech Republic. Members of the Moravian Church settled at Fulneck in 1744. They were descendants of old Bohemian/Czech Unity of the Brethren (extinct after 1620 due to forcible re-Catholization imposed on the Czech lands by Habsburg emperors), which in 1722 had found refuge in Saxony on the estate of Nicolaus Ludwig Count von Zinzendorf. Within the next few years after settling, housing, as well as a school and a chapel, were built. The chapel building was completed in 1748. In 1753 and 1755 the Boys' and Girls' Schools were opened.

Many of the 18th-century stone houses in the village are listed buildings. Cricketer Sir Leonard Hutton, who played for Yorkshire and England was born in Fulneck. Hutton still holds the record for the highest innings (364) by an Englishman in a test match. H. H. Asquith, Prime Minister of the United Kingdom 1908-16 and Diana Rigg, the actress famous for appearing in The Avengers both attended Fulneck School.

Now you leave Bankhouse and take Scholebrooke Lane down the valley towards The Banks and Black Carr Woods. Upon reaching the valley bottom the track narrows considerably and becomes no more than a footpath. It snakes along the side of Tyersal Beck through ancient Black Carr Woods on one side and The Banks on the other.

Black Carr Woods is the only wooded area in the Bradford area which is situated on coal geology as opposed to the otherwise predominate Gritstone. The shallow valley you are now crossing is drained by Carr Beck and Pudsey Beck. This area is considered to be one of the most natural Oak and Birch woodlands in the United Kingdom. Amongst the other tree species that grow wild here are Alder and Willow. Here the woods are silent apart from only the occasional distant birdcall as you walk immersed in the secluded peacefulness of the place.

You continue to walk through the wood until you come to a stone railway bridge and its abutment. This lonely stone structure stretches over a redundant railway cutting. This track was installed in 1875 after much negotiation with several railway companies. Until this point, the growing population associated with the cloth manufacturing industry in Pudsey had been dependent upon their nearest station at Stanningley.

In 1870, a local committee was formed to petition the London and North-Western Railway Company to continue their line from Wortley to Bradford via Pudsey. The request was, however, declined on account of the difficulties of crossing the Tong valley and obtaining a site on which to build a station at Bradford.

The committee was determined and took their appeal instead to the Lancashire and Yorkshire Railway Company. The application was favourably received, but during the surveying of the land for construction, the Great Northern Railway Company also obtained permission in parliament to branch from their Leeds-Bradford line to Pudsey. Further negotiations ensued, and after consultation with thirty-two landowners, a route was agreed.

The ceremony of the first cutting took place on the 24th March 1875 and the railway opened for passenger traffic on the 1st April 1878. Two hundred feet to your left the track passed through a tunnel on its way to Greenside Station. The track was finally dismantled in 1964 as part of the Reshaping of British Railways, or the 'Beeching Axe' as it is sometimes known. Oh Doctor Beeching what have you done?

After passing by two small disused quarries you emerge at the side of The Fox and Grapes pub on Smalewell Road. From here it is but a short walk to the main Waterloo Road in Pudsey where you can catch the bus to either Bradford or Leeds to conclude your journey.

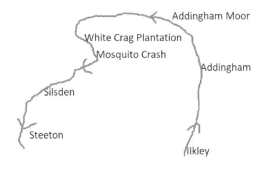

This walk begins in the centre of Addingham village and to reach there you have to take theX84/85 or 62 bus from Ilkey. To reach the former spa town of Ilkley you have to take a train from either Leeds or Bradford. The approximate distance for this walk is 6.2 miles.

Once in Addingham you head towards the old Roman road on the moors above the village. Addingham nestles in a pocket by the Wharfe with a plethora of paths heading off in all directions towards the uplands. It is an ancient settlement, founded by the Saxons of the dark Ages – its name means "the place of Adda's people".

Addingham's long agricultural heritage gave way – in the eighteenth century - to a more prosperous future through the foresight of one man, John Cunliffe (1742-1813). Cunliffe, a yeoman farmer, moved with the times during the Industrial Revolution by establishing a worsted spinning mill, Low Mill, now demolished, in 1787.

Up to that time, weaving and spinning had been a cottage industry and evidence of this is still to be found in the back streets of Addingham where a number of three-storey houses survive, the top floor being taken over by the workers. Another mill, High Mill, followed and by the 1830s the two establishments were employing a workforce of three hundred. High Mill, situated by the Wharfe just north of the village, still stands and has been converted into houses.

The Roman road or Moor Lane as it is known today is just about the only evidence of the three hundred and fifty years of the Roman occupation of this area. The first part of Moor Lane is lined by sleepy suburban semi-detached houses. This changes at the junction of Turner Lane as the road becomes no more than a footpath. From here the vista is more pastoral as you cross the Addingham Wharfedale Road and head towards the open moor.

You are making for a spot only some five hundred metres along the old Roman road to where you climb over the high stone wall on your left and walk along a line of circumvallation to an Iron-Age settlement known as Round Dikes Camp.

When you get on the moor there are no discernible signs of the encampment as it is only visible from the air, only a faint circular area can be seen. From here you may gain a feeling of great admiration for the people that once lived out in this windswept and lonely location. From this commanding position on the summit of Counter Hill, you can see your next destination some distance away in front of you almost.. Across the old drover's road of Parson Lane and Marchup Plantation the faint outline of a tall stone tower comes into view. It stands like a beacon enticing you to journey towards it across the moorland, just as it had done to many others since its construction in the 1850s.

This sighting or survey tower was built by engineers during the construction of nearby Silsden Reservoir and the associated Barden Aqueduct, a three-arch span at Swartha Wood on the eastern fringe of Silsden.

Crossing the summit and dropping down towards Parson Lane takes some energy and effort as the terrain is quite steep. Here high sided stone walls line the lane and serve to keep the nearby sheep in place. From this point it is only a few minutes walking to reach Cringles Lane close to High Marchup Farm.

The sighting tower is only about a quarter of a mile away now so continue to head in that direction. When you reach it you must walk for a short distance up Bolton Road then turn right along Lippersly Lane. Passing the old quarries of Brooks Hill, you continue towards White Crag Plantation and the area known as Windgate Nick. The lane rises gently as you pass the beautiful cottages of Lower Hang Goose and the farm of Upper Hang Goose. This was just as far as you need to go as you now take a track on your left up the moors to the old quarries of Old Nab and White Crag Plantation behind it.

White Crag and its adjacent Plantation is hemmed in on the north side by a giant of a stone wall. Apart from the occasional loose top stone this marvellous testament to human endeavour, will and spirit stands today just as it did the day it was constructed two centuries ago. You follow this wall until it turns to your right and takes you to a spot where Pilot Sgt John Hudson Staples and navigator Sgt Ralph Ernest Andrews lost their lives in 1943.

On March 23rd, 1943 at approximately 9.00 pm an RAF MKII de Haviland Mosquito aircraft (affectionately known as the wooden wonder) DD750 of 25 squadron RAF Church Fenton crashed into the hillside near to Windgate Nick on Addingham High Moor. The plane was returning to base at Church Fenton after a cancelled "Ranger" operation. The "Ranger" operations were similar to the Luftwaffe intruder flights, night-fighters would fly alone in the landing patterns of enemy aircraft near their bases and try and shoot them down.

The squadron the Mosquito belonged to had been using a forward base of Coltishall airfield and three aircraft took off from there to return to base at Church Fenton on this evening.

On nearing Church Fenton, the crew contacted base to state their intention of landing but were told to hold off the landing and await their turn in the airfield circuit. They were wrongly directed into a holding pattern over high ground and were then given the wrong height at which to fly. The aircraft flew into the high ground to the east of Silsden at speed and at night in low cloud conditions.

The aircraft then somersaulted over the moorland ridge finally coming to rest against the stone wall which divides a field and White Crag Plantation. Unfortunately, the two crew were killed and their bodies were found lying together a short distance from the main wreckage on the opposite side of the wall.

The aircraft was returning from RAF Coltishall in Norfolk to its home base at RAF Church Fenton near York. Why it was flying twenty-eight miles west of its base is unclear but from local reports the aircraft had already circled and was thought to be searching for recognisable landmarks. One of the wings of the plane had come to rest against the stone wall which divides the field from the White Crag Plantation.

Today no trace of the accident remains and the only evidence that anything at all happened on this windswept spot is the stone memorial to the two airmen that died. The stone wall was repaired and the gorse and heather was reborn and renewed long ago.

To leave this place you continue the route along the wall till it dips down towards White Crag Moor before crossing Jerry Lane and take a footpath onto Brunthwaite Lane. This track winds through the hamlets of High Brunthwaite and then Brunthwaite itself, before becoming Howden Road. The shining rooftops of Silsden are now in view.

Silsden is generally an agricultural area, the industry came with the canal and the Industrial Revolution. The town hosted a number of mills none of which now operate in their original form. There is still some industry in the town, some in old mill buildings and some in a new industrial estate between the town and the river. During the 1940s a hostel was built off Howden Road, (now a housing estate)

The hostel housed refugees and prisoners of war from various countries and various camps. A plaque to commemorate this is located at the bottom of Ings Way, at the entrance to the housing estate. But perhaps Silsden's most bizarre claim to fame was when The Guinness Book of World Records reported that the biggest onion ever, at 14 lb, was grown in Silsden in 2010 by Vincent Throup. However this has since been beaten and his wife has allowed him to return to sleeping in the marital bed.

Walking along Keighley Road towards Steeton it is not long before you come to Silsden's old Police Station on the right. Opened in 1902 it is now a private dwelling but has not always been so because in 1911 it was attacked by rioting villagers. A very unpopular policeman had been too enthusiastic in his duties and a popular local man was arrested.

Considerable damage was caused to the police station with officers actually hiding under their desks, and questions were raised in the House of Commons. The policeman was removed from the town and no more trouble occurred and the village returned to its sleepy little self.

But this period of calm does not last because in 1914 Harry Rawson becomes the first Silsden soldier to be sent to the front. The following year marks the funeral of Ben Hodgson, the first Silsden soldier killed in action. Silent crowds lined the street in respect as his funeral cortege passed along the street that he knew so well.

Villagers are now meeting every day in the Town Hall to make 'comforts' for the men on the Western Front. Also in 1915, the first Belgian war refugees arrive in Silsden and are accommodated by local families. When the war ends in 1918, 106 young men with Silsden connections (home and work) have lost their lives. They include three Faulkner brothers from Bridge Street. Another Faulkner brother, suffering from grief and shell-shock, is committed to Menston Asylum where he remained until his death in 1971.

Keighley Road continues to lead you away from Silsden itself and before long you cross the River Aire. From here Steeton railway station is but a short walk across the new bypass. Here you can catch a well-deserved train back to Shipley and beyond to Bradford or Leeds to complete this walk.

Denholme to Bingley via Harden

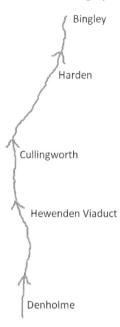

Bingley

Harden

Cullingworth

Hewenden Viaduct

Denholme

The village of Denholme is reached from Bradford or Keighley by the number 67 bus. The approximate distance for this walk is 5.1 miles.

The Victorians were quite an impressive brand of people. They ushered in a great age of innovation, expansion, social and military expansion which made Great Britain the greatest and most powerful country on Earth. They created an empire like no other before or since. The area around Bradford is steeped in the Victorian influence as the districts many fine buildings and structures prove. It is one of these fine structures that this walk is centred upon. It is situated out in the green and pleasant countryside surrounding Bradford, and it is to here that you travel to start your journey to pay homage to surely one of the local Victorian's finest architectural legacies.

Denholme is just the same as the other villages in these parts that were created by local wool barons and industrialists. Like the villages of Saltaire and nearby Queensbury, Denholme still has the shadow of its creator and benefactor hanging over it. One only has to look at the names of many of the streets and even the park to appreciate the impact that the Foster family had on the village and its people.

The entire Victorian housing sites of Denholme were built by the Fosters who also built the old textile mills in the village. The houses were constructed for the workers of the mills. It was common in Victorian England for wealthy businessmen to build entire towns to house the workers of their mills.

The village sits astride the old Roman Road from Manchester to Ilkley, though there is no evidence of any settlement there. The line of the road is visible on the ground to the south of the village, not far from St Paul's church. The first evidence of habitation in the area dates from the 13th century.

There is a grant of land, dated 1239, whereby Thomas de Thornton gave grazing land at Denholme to the monks of Byland Abbey. It is likely that the monks would have built a Grange in the area and this may well have given the village its first occupants. The Monks grazed sheep as fleeces were a valuable cash crop at the time. By the 15th century, the land belonged to the Tempest family who held it for many years until it was gambled in a game of cards and lost to The Saville family of Halifax by Sir Richard Tempest.

In 1822, the main occupations in the village were mining, farming and handloom weaving. Coal, fire clay, iron pyrates and York stone could be found in reasonably plentiful supply and there were good sources of water. These natural resources attracted industrial interest, and the Foster's arrived on the scene. Recognising the economic potential of the village they started building their mill on the only level plateau of land available in the valley, with easy access to water. The first mill was started in 1838 but was never completed. It was blown down in January 1839. The second was larger than the original and was a profitable concern until it burnt down in 1857, a common fate for these industrial buildings

The third mill, larger still, also thrived, but on September 6th, 1873, there was a strike which lasted 14 days. An agreement, to employ only weavers in the new shed, which held 1,000 looms, had been broken, leading to industrial action. In 2005, any employment on the site of the old mill ended with the closure of Pennine Fibres. The mill building has subsequently been demolished.

Today the village is quiet and pretty much of a backwater in places. Many if not all of the 18th century former workers cottages survive and are inhabited by local people.

The small local bus from Bradford to Keighley will drop you in the centre of the village. It is from here that you begin this walk by striding confidently along the main road through the village. Passing by rows of sturdy workers cottages huddled by the roadside, you head towards your ultimate goal of Bingley. But Bingley is miles away and there is much of the local landscape and history to enjoy before you reach the ancient market town in the valley below.

After a short walk you turn off the main road and take the narrow track to your right named Carr Lane. This will lead you past Carr House Farm and onwards towards the former Halifax, Keighley and Thornton railway line. This lane is a dead end with a tiny cottage right at the end. Next to it is a stream and this small area conjures up a vision of pastoral remoteness.

It is actually a small farmstead with a tiny cottage tucked away at the side. The stream is no more than a spring which emanates from the field a few yards from the cottage. The old G.N.R railway line used to run but a short distance from this tranquil place and the cottage would have shaken like the barley in the wind when the trains roared past.

Turning back you make your way up the lane and take a small footpath to your right which will lead you across the fields to nearby Whalley Lane. Here the path crosses the site of a tiny delph. The scarring of the landscape is evidence of the toil and the backbreaking work of the tough local men who raped the land for a living.

From here you can clearly see the line of thick trees that now grow along the former train line. Nature always reclaims the land once man has finished with it even if it sometimes takes many years.

Climbing over the drystone wall onto Whalley Lane you drop onto the tarmac and cross the road towards Buck Park Farm and head towards Hewenden viaduct. The famed viaduct is the main reason for this walk. Like the other viaduct on this former train line at Thornton, it is now part of the Sustrans railway trail and can be enjoyed in a way that the Victorians never intended when they constructed.

The narrow lane winds down the hillside flanked by open fields to both sides and the trees of the trackbed stand proudly up ahead. Here the lane passes under the train bed via a road bridge. This small but tall bridge with its twin abutments was built to allow the railway line to cross Whalley Lane. Even though the road is but a mere country lane, the Victorian engineers designed and constructed this bridge with as much care and attention to detail as they had when they constructed nearby Hewenden viaduct and other such structures along the line.

Perhaps stand for a moment to admire this humble bridge and revel in the detail that the fine Victorians took a to a new level when they laid their railways all those years ago.

You now follow the lane as it snakes around the valley bottom to cross Denholme Beck at Meal Bridge. Here the beck is wide and powerful and certainly would have had to have been to power the sawmill that once stood in Park Wood nearby. Close to Park Wood was Buck Park Quarry so perhaps it may have been stone and not timber that the mill processed.

Nearby there is a small track which leads off Whalley Lane and this will lead you through the woods towards Hewenden Reservoir and the viaduct beyond. Look up ahead and just above the treetops you can see the ridge of the viaduct. It stands perhaps half a mile away. Here the track skirts along the edge of the woods and underneath yet another fine old railway bridge and through the light covering of trees. This will be a welcome change after the recent dense and heavy wooded areas that you have tramped through. The scenery is light and airy as you pass the house of Wood Nook. What a splendid place to live, isolated amongst the trees with the reservoir on the doorstep.

The fields sweep down the towards the water's edge of the reservoir as cattle graze all around. You now head towards the site of Wilsden railway station. Built in 1886 for The Great Northern Railway it is actually two miles from Wilsden and closer to Harecroft. It closed in 1955 and only the Station Masters house survives today as a private residence.

Climb up the banking above the fields towards the former station site and from here you can look down upon the magnificent 1.16 Kilometre long Hewenden Reservoir. Here the sun shimmers on the water's surface as Whooper Swans and Yellow-Legged Gulls fly overhead. The magnificence of the reservoir is so captivating that you may hardly notice the viaduct standing guard away to the north. The pleasure of striding along its high seventeen arches is yet to come.

Crossing Hewenden Beck, the viaduct stands at 123 feet tall and spans 576 yards with 17 arches each of 16.5 yards. The viaduct originally formed part of the Keighley and Thornton Branch of the Great Northern Railway and, together with the mile-long Lees Moor Tunnel, opened to passenger trains in 1883. Engineered by Richard Johnson from Hammer-dressed and rock-faced stone, it served as a railway viaduct along the Queensbury Lines and it now forms part of the Great Northern Railway Trail for cyclists and walkers.

This grand structure is a Grade II listed and due to shifting sands in the earth below the foundations go as deep as the height of the structure. It was constructed from stone prised from the ground in the nearby Manywells quarry. The last locomotive traffic crossed this superb structure in 1963, and since then many thousands of people have walked its length high up in the sky. Today it is your turn.

As you open the gate at the East end you may have no sense of the length of the structure due to the curve which was built into it. It is almost like a massive stone banana and was built this way due to the topography of the land below. The stonework was unaltered by the passing years, the surface and corners as sharp as the day they were cut by the Victorian stonemason's skilled hands.

Standing there looking down upon the wide expanse of rolling fields and hills you may wonder if the men that built it ever considered they were creating something that will surely last a thousand years. When you reach the far end you will find a small area with an information board that tells the story of the viaduct and affords you a view back along its whole length.

From here you can truly appreciate the viaducts stunning architecture as the seventeen arches unfold across the valley below you. From here it is easy to imagine the dense clouds of steam pumping from the locomotives funnel as it swept majestically around the bend towards nearby Cullingworth station.

Now you rejoin the trail on the former railway bed and you will soon arrive at the site of the former Cullingworth station. Cullingworth railway station was a station on the Queensbury Lines which ran between Keighley, Bradford, and Halifax. The station served the village of Cullingworth, West Yorkshire, England.

Opening for passengers in 1884 and closing in May 1955 it carried goods traffic until 1963 when the surviving line closed completely. Today nothing remains apart from some modern buildings on the site of a former goods warehouse. You now move on through the village towards the open road which runs to Harden. Take Halifax Road past the Vicarage and its ancient stone horse drinking trough. As in Denholme earlier, the road is lined with early 18th-century mill workers cottages.

Cullingworth itself stands in the eastern foothills of the South Pennines. Manywells Beck flows through the village, leading into Harden Beck, a small tributary of the River Aire. The centre of the village still retains a distinctly rural feel, despite the extensive 20th-century residential development around the older core. The original core of the village, located on Station Road and Georges Square, contains many listed vernacular structures. These include farmhouses, converted barns, and commercial buildings as well as smaller cottages.

The more formal style of architecture of the church and chapels provide an interesting civic aspect. These buildings all provide a unique record of the early development of Cullingworth into a thriving agricultural hamlet and later into a busy cloth-manufacturing village.

Several other mills were built in and around Cullingworth. A Corn Mill and Tannery were active at Cow House Fold, to the northeast of the village during this period. However, the largest mill in the area, constructed by 1852, was the Worsted mill on the western side of Halifax Road. This mill, built around a courtyard with an unusual gate and entrance, was run by the Townend Brothers, an eminent and wealthy local family.

The mill was extended in 1823, 1840 and again in 1860 and was the first maker of Worsted heald yarns in the Bradford district as well becoming the main source of employment in the village, at its peak employing 800 workers. The Townend family also worked the coal pits at Denholme, Dene Brow, Hazel Crook and Hollin Hall. These collieries supplied high-grade coal for the gas works, which were located within the Cullingworth Mills complex and supplied gas not only to the mill but to the whole village.

People were attracted to the village to find employment in the mills and during the 19th century, the population of Cullingworth expanded. This increase necessitated the construction of more buildings, mostly in the form of back-to-back and terraced housing. The settlement developed southwards towards Cullingworth Gate and east of Halifax Road. Improvements were undertaken in the village such as the widening of the roads (including Station Road) and the demolition of some older properties. Today part of the giant expanse of Cullingworth Mill survives along with the foreman's house and the entrance lodge.

As you drop down the hill into the gully alongside Ellar Carr Beck take care as the road is steep and there are no pavements. But after a short distance a pavement does appear and you can relax. The road is lined with the dense woodland of Ellar Beck on one side and a large earth banking on the other as you make your way towards the cottages of Cow House Bridge in the gully bottom. This short row of former workers cottages is pristine in appearance belying their great age. Built to house the workers in the nearby mill Woodfield Mill, they were now homes to local people who commuted into nearby Bingley and Bradford to make their living.

Bingley Road now becomes Hill End Lane as it sweeps uphill towards Hunters Hill and the site of a former Tannery at Hunters Hill Farm. Catstones Moor, with its ancient quarry and even more ancient Ring stones stands guard above you on the left. The road is long and straight as it winds up the side of the moor towards Harden. The almost square plantation of Hunters Hill Wood appeared to my left besides Catstones Moor and over to your right are the open meadows and fields towards Wilsden.

After perhaps two miles of slogging up the hill, you enter the edge of the village of Harden. Passing Leech Lane where excavations in the 1980s suggested a Roman settlement and villa once stood, you descend the slight gradient into Harden itself.

The main road through the village is once again lined with pristine former mill workers cottages. Every summer the village holds a medieval "fayre", with jugglers, jousting, and other entertainments. Medieval tents are set up on the top field and demonstrations show how simple tasks like the washing up and making a tent peg would have been done.

The long straight road passes very close to the famous St. Ives Estate as it winds its way down towards Bingley. The St. Ives area is known to have been inhabited from at least the Neolithic or Bronze Age from artefacts that remain. Up until the Dissolution of the Monasteries in 1540, the land was divided between the monks of Rievaulx Abbey and Drax Priory. In 1540 the land was purchased by a Walter Paslew and was subsequently owned by the Laycock and Milner families and the St. Ives mansion house was built in 1616.

In 1635 the Ferrands purchased St. Ives at the time known as Harden Grange, and it was in 1858 that the names of Harden Grange and the local St. Ives were interchanged. There are stories of a local connection with General Fairfax and the Civil War, but little is known with any certainty. Sarah Busfield (née Ferrand) inherited St. Ives from her uncle and she and her son William changed their family name to Ferrand and when she died in 1854 her son William Busfield Ferrand inherited the property. The estate and mansion were bought by Bingley Urban District Council in 1929.

A granite obelisk close to Lady Blantyre's Rock north-west of Coppice Pond commemorates the career of William Busfield Ferrand (1809–89), a Member of Parliament, magistrate and one-time owner of St. Ives Estate. Coppice Pond was built as a feed water supply for what is thought originally to be a fulling mill, later landscaped by the Ferrands and used for boating. Today it is stocked with a variety of fish for angling and has a bird hide and duck feeding pier.

On the north side of the pond is the archery club while east of Coppice Pond is the mill. A mill has been recorded on this site since the early 14th century and it is probably the oldest building on the estate, although modified since then. To the south of Coppice Pond near Cuckoo Nest Cottages is the restored Baxter's Pond, fed by both Coppice Pond and the mill.

East of the mill is Home Farm with its cafe, coach house, and stables, and to the rear a Dutch barn and a car park.

The road now begins to descend down the hill between Bell Bank Wood and Holme House Wood. The ancient and historic Ireland Bridge and the small town of Bingley are now not far away. Perhaps you may have time for a well-kept pint of local beer in the famed Brown Cow public house on Ireland Bridge itself.

You can catch any number of buses in Bingley town centre which will take you to Shipley and then beyond to wherever your final destination may be.

Outlane To Rishworth Via Scammonden

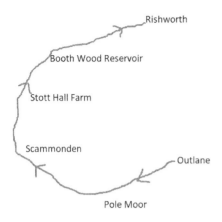

To begin this walk you catch 536/537 bus from either Halifax or Huddersfield depending on your location. The approximate distance for this walk is 7.0 miles.

This walk begins at the junction of Stainland Road and New Hey Road. From here you walk away from the village along New Hey Road itself which runs parallel to the M62 Motorway and for the first thousand yards or so covers the supposed site of a Roman Road and fort at nearby Slack.

The site of the fort was on gently sloping ground sheltered by a hill rising to 1,200 feet above sea level about four miles from Huddersfield. Observation posts on the surrounding hills commanded views towards Blackstone Edge, Standedge, Huddersfield and the Stainland Valley in the Halifax direction. The fort was occupied until about ad 140 and today nothing remains.

As you pass Gosport Lane on your right look out for the present-day house directly opposite. This was once a Beerhouse named Captain's Arms.

A beerhouse was a type of public house created in the United Kingdom by the 1830 Beerhouse Act, legally defined as a place "where beer is sold to be consumed on the premises". Existing public houses were issued with licences by local magistrates under the terms of the Retail Brewers Act 1828, and were subject to police inspections at any time of the day or night.

Proprietors of the new beerhouses, on the other hand, simply had to buy a licence from the government costing two guineas per annum, equivalent to about £150 as of 2010. Until the Wine and Beerhouse Act 1869 gave local magistrates the authority to renew beerhouse licences, the two classes of establishment were in direct competition.

Continue to walk along New Hey Road towards Marsden Gate passing by roadside weavers cottages and tastefully restored roadside farmhouses. Soon the road crosses over the fast-flowing M62 Motorway and heads towards Pole Moor. The last three hundred yards on the Outlane side had to be diverted to accommodate the motorway.

Almost immediately you pass by The Lower Royal George public house, which may or may not be currently trading, and then soon after former Upper Royal George which was renamed The Jack O' Mitre and again which may or not be trading depending on local economic conditions.

Just after the junction with Pole Moor you turn right down Hey Lane whilst noticing the roadside house named Clay House which was once another former Beerhouse named The Globe Inn. After two hundred yards on the right is yet another tastefully converted roadside farmhouse named New House. Hey Lane continues downhill to cross the motorway before carrying on towards Stainland Dean, but long before then you turn left along Pinfold Lane and head towards the massive Scammonden Reservoir.

Passing by the farmhouses of Camp Hill and Green Slacks you soon arrive on a plateau overlooking the famous reservoir. You may wish to rest awhile here at this spot as it affords a magnificent view of the reservoir below you.

Scammonden Reservoir or Dam is part of the M62 motorway between junctions 22 and 23, the only such structure in Britain. Its construction by the Ministry of Transport and Huddersfield Corporation Waterworks required the passing of the Huddersfield Corporation Act 1965. The motorway dam spans the Deanhead Valley in the Pennines between Huddersfield and Rochdale and the main contractor for the project was Sir Alfred McAlpine & Sons.

The area of the water surface when the reservoir is full is 42 hectares. The level of the bellmouth overflow above sea level is 252 metres (827 ft). The reservoir holds 7800 million litres. Its length is 1.4 kilometres.

Deanhead village was submerged and many buildings demolished to make way for the reservoir but the church remains and its vicarage is used by the sailing club. Both the church and adjacent school were at risk of slipping down the hillside into the dam and were not used after 1971 when the motorway opened. The church was renovated in 2002 and the old schoolhouse has been converted into a private dwelling.

Surveying began in November 1961 and the route of the carriageway was determined in mid 1963. Excavation in the Deanhead Valley commenced the following year and for the dam in 1966. This required the removal of 713,000 cubic metres of peat bog to reach the solid rock base nearly 13 metres below ground level. Material excavated elsewhere on the line of the motorway, clay from cuttings between Lofthouse and Gildersome, and 3.4 million cubic metres from the Deanhead excavations was used to build the dam's embankment which is 625 metres in length and 63.1 metres above the original valley floor. The 3.6 million cubic metre embankment is 435 metres wide at its base and 55 metres at road level.

Scammonden Water is 51.8 metres at its deepest point and water is drawn-off through a 2.5 kilometre tunnel driven southwards to supply Huddersfield. The overflow bellmouth, next to the valve shaft superstructure, discharges water to the valley below via a tunnel in the valley on the reservoir's eastern side.

The reservoir started to fill in July 1969 and the area was landscaped and parking and other facilities were provided. The motorway, which was dependent on the completion of the dam, was opened to traffic on 20 December 1970 and officially opened by HM Queen Elizabeth II who unveiled a plaque near the valve tower of Scammonden Water on 14 October 1971.

The submerged village of Dean Head itself was a township covering more than 2,000 acres. In 1806 the village had a population of 453. In the 1870s it had a church, a Baptist chapel, a national school, a post office and 190 houses. Industry in the village included cotton-spinning and woollen manufacture and there were freestone quarries. There had been a chapel in Scammonden since 1615 and it was a chapelry in the Huddersfield ecclesiastical parish. Its old chapel was rebuilt at a cost of £1000 in 1813 before being replaced by the church in 1865.

There is more than one footpath that you can take to make your way around the reservoir towards St. Bartholomew's church high up on the far bank. Once you have reached the church you carry on along Church Lane and before long this country lane joins with Saddleworth Road at Moselden Heights. Here you turn left and continue along Saddleworth Road until you reach the farmhouse named The Delight which is opposite the turning to New lane.

From here you must trek across the short expanse of Moselden Heights, which in the spring and summer is inhabited by many sheep, before descending down the far side towards the motorway and the strange farm that sits between the two carriageways.

This farm named Stott Hall Farm is renowned the world over due to its unusual and quirky position. Stott Hall Farm made national headlines in the 1960s when the M62 was built and has been a focal point ever since. Owned by Yorkshire Water it was thought the farm in Yorkshire would have to be demolished but a quirk in the land's geology saved it.

Built in the 18th century on Moss Moor, Stott Hall Farm is the only farm in the UK situated in the middle of a motorway. It lies south of Booth Wood Reservoir where the carriageways are separated between junctions 22 and 23. The road divides for much of its length between the Windy Hill and Deanhead cuttings because of the surrounding geography but a myth persists that it was split because the owners Ken and Beth Wild refused to sell.

There is an access tunnel beneath each carriageway of the motorway and you need to navigate both of these to resume your journey on the far side where you continue downhill towards the massive overflow wall of Booth Wood Reservoir.

Booth Wood Reservoir is a man-made upland reservoir that lies north of the M62 motorway and south of the A672 road near to Rishworth and Ripponden. The reservoir was approved for construction in 1966 and completed in 1971. It supplies water to Wakefield. The reservoir dams the Booth Dean Clough watercourse and takes water directly from the surrounding moorland. It has a plain concrete crest on the dam head which is straight and extends to a length of 1,150 feet and a height of 157 feet

In 1995 a long dry spell in the summer created a larger than normal abstraction of water from Booth Wood creating the need to transport water into the reservoir as stocks ran very low. Road tankers carrying freshwater were despatched from Selby in North Yorkshire and Kielder Water in Northumberland to bring water for offloading at Booth Wood. At the height of the operation, 700 tankers delivered 70,000 tonnes of water a day to the reservoir which then fed other reservoirs in West Yorkshire.

On 14 August 2016, the A672 road which runs along the northern edge of the reservoir was closed whilst police searched for a driver and car that had plunged off the road and into the reservoir. The driver was believed to be the only person in the car and the search operation involved helicopters and underwater divers. The search resumed the next day when a man's body was recovered.

The track in front of the overflow wall leads to Moselden Lane where, in the area where the road bends after two hundred yards, Booth Wood Mill once stood. This road leads to Oldham Road after a short distance and here you bare right and continue along through Booth Wood, Turner Wood and alongside Booth Dean Clough until you reach the village of Rishworth where you can catch the bus back into Halifax to complete this walk.

Monk Fryston To Church Fenton

This walk begins with a bus journey from Leeds to Monk Fryston (402/403) and the approximate distance is 5.1 miles.

It is a bit of a trek as it is strictly speaking in North Yorkshire but well worth it to tramp along through the vast open wheat and beet filled meadows of the far side of West Yorkshire.

The bus will deposit you opposite The crown on main Street in Monk Fryston. The Dictionary of British Place Names notes Monk Fryston as "Fristun" (c.1030) and "Munechesfryston" (1166). The name derives from the Old English for "farmstead of the Frisians", with prefix 'Monk' relating to it being an 11th-century possession of Selby Abbey.

The name of the village originates from Monk's Free Stone as all of the stone used to build Selby Abbey was obtained from a quarry in the centre of the village across the road from the old school building. The quarry was filled in for a housing development located next to the new school building, built on the old school field in 1998-99.

The old school building has since been converted to housing. The village has one public house, The Crown Inn, which dates back to the 1600s, and a hotel, the Monk Fryston Hall Hotel which dates back to the 12th century.

The National Heritage List for England, compiled by English Heritage, holds 15 listed buildings for Monk Fryston. The list includes the Grade I St Wilfrid's Church, the Grade II Monk Fryston Hall and two Grade II milestones. The York and North Midland Railway passes to the west of the village. An old station platform still exists next to the railway just down from the South Milford sidings.

   The peacefull almost sleepy feeling that you may experience is fueled by the stillness and the almost total absence of traffic along the main street. This may be only shattered by the occasional muck spreading tractor, and this will be reserved for the nearby fields but the aroma leaves you in no doubt that you are in the countryside.

   You walk along Main Street until it joins with Lumby Lane and in no time you arrive at the junction with Ingthorpe lane where you turn right. The blackberry bush lined lane leads you alongside the railway line and after five hundred yards you again turn right to walk around the back of the former deer park for Monk Fryston Hall.

   Monk Fryston Hall is a Grade II listed country house standing in 66 acres of mature parkland. The hall was originally built for Selby Abbey in the 13th century in magnesian limestone with a stone slate roof. It was heavily restored circa 1740, altered again in 1897 and an additional range added in the 20th century. The hall was bought in 1680 by the Hemsworth family and the family occupied the hall for several generations. In 1946 it was sold to an S.W. Tinsdale who converted the hall to a hotel, selling it on in 1954 to the Duke of Rutland. After changing hands twice since then it is now being run as a luxury hotel known as Monk Fryston Hall Hotel.

   After some six hundred yards you come to Turpin Lane where you turn left and begin to cross Ingthornes Drain and Lumby Common. Here the vista is filled with bare ploughed fields to each side but in the middle distance you may spot the telltale signs of Sugar Beet crowns. This is where most of the sugar you put in your tea originates not the West Indies.

   To cultivate Sugar Beet successfully the land must be properly prepared. Deep ploughing is the first principle of beet cultivation. It allows the roots to penetrate the subsoil with little obstruction and this may explain the empty ploughed fields depending on the season of course.

Passing by Milford Grange the track is soon swallowed up by the sea of beet the reddy-brown bodies of this simple plant offering itself up for your inspection as you walk by.

Here, in the middle distance you will see an imposing red brick building, its tower looms into view as you approach it. The long line of rail freight carriages standing silently on the track beside only serve to add to the desolation of the area. This is Milford East junction where there once stood a station just down the line from here. This closed on the 1st of Octobre 1904 with the station buildings being demolished in 1960. Today, the site remains in operation for locomotive swapping.

The massive industrial building is a former Malthouse and although appearing disused and forlorn is still in use as industrial units. A Malthouse is a building where cereal grain is converted into malt by soaking it in water, allowing it to sprout then drying it to prevent further growth. The Malt is used in the brewing of beer, whiskey and certain foods. The traditional Malthouse was phased out during the twentieth century in favour of more mechanised production.

Once past the former Malthouse continue along Turpin Lane for a short distance before turning left along Common Lane until it meets the A162. From here you now turn right and walk along the road as it passes by Sherburn In Elmet Airfield. In the 1920s, the Yorkshire Aeroplane Club began operating here. The novelist, pilot, and aeronautical engineer Nevil Shute was a member, and on the club's management committee. At the time, the club was flying de Havilland Moths. In his memoir, Slide Rule, Shute records that " the Yorkshire Club quickly attracted a fair cross-section of young Yorkshire men and women, so that a Sunday spent at the Club was a merry Sunday." He also met his future wife, Frances Mary Heaton, a physician, at the club. After establishing Airspeed Ltd., an aircraft manufacturing firm, he personally flew the first two test flights of the company's first aircraft here. It was a glider, known as the Tern, and was launched using a "very old Buick car" pulling a steel cable.

During the Second World War the airfield was used as a Royal Air Force station. From 1940 Blackburn Aircraft used a Ministry of Aircraft Production factory here to build 1699 Fairey Swordfish naval torpedo aircraft.

The Airborne Forces Experimental Establishment (AFEE) was moved from RAF Ringway to Sherburn on 17 June 1942. It was charged with developing the means to deploy allied airborne forces and supplies on operations by Military glider, Parachute and other means. The AFEE moved to RAF Beaulieu on 4 January 1945.

Post-war, Sherburn has been used by private pilots and by aero clubs for training and leisure flying. The Yorkshire Aeroplane Club was based here for many years and organised several international air rallies in the early 1950s.

After traversing the A162 for a while you reach a large roundabout and here you turn right then after only a few yards turn left along Fenton Lane past Sherburn In Elmet Railway Station. This is not a station as such more of a simple halt with no facilities. Passing by the former Sherburn Brick and Tile works you continue along Fenton lane. Here the road is long, straight and lined with large verges.

Apart from the massive British Gypsum factory to your right, buildings are scarce in this flat rolling landscape. Sherburn Common Farm and Fenton Common Farm stand by on the right just as they have done for centuries their view uninterrupted by the expansive fields. At the turnoff for Little Fenton the lane becomes Ash Lane and from here it is only a short distance to your final destination of the village of Church Fenton. You are now on Fenton Common and here the fields are alive with their life-giving gifts of Wheat.

As you round the final bend in Ash Lane, Church End Farm welcomes you into the village. The red brick and stone buildings centred around the enclosed farmyard appear just as they would have done two centuries ago. Likewise the church and graveyard of St. Mary's a little further along the lane. This church is reputed to be one of the smallest completely cruciform churches in the country that carries such a large tower.

Constructed from stone frm the huddleston quarry nearby, the North and sections of the East transept date from 1230. The first recorded vicar was Thomas de Fenton in 1338. The tower was added in 1240 and the church has undergone two recent major restorations in 1844 and 1966. The original church clock was removed into the tower in 1780 but it was replaced a year later by a new clock purchased from Goodall of Aberford. Parts of this clock remain in the current mechanism.

The original vicarage of the church is the present "old vicarage" opposite the Methodist chapel which dates from at least 1663. The new vicarage was built in 1870 near the train station on land purchased from The North Eastern Railway Company.

The name Church Fenton means a village with a church in fen or marshland. The village was recorded along with nearby Little Fenton as Fentun in the Domesday book of 1086. The name Church Fenton has evolved over the years, and the name Kirk Fenton (Kirk= church) is first mentioned in 1338 signifying the establishment of a church in the village. The word "Ton" or "Tun" suggests a community within an enclosure which has been reclaimed from the fen which is an old English word for a marsh.

It is likely that the origins of the village were agricultural, although in 1400 records show that many villagers were employed at the Huddleston stone quarry at a time when the stone was being used in the construction of York Cathedral. In 1458 the village had a population of 42 married couples,26 single adults and one tradesman(Blacksmith) there appears to be no mention of any children.

Major drainage work opened up the village for agriculture between the years 1600 and 1800. Of course the village is best known today for its association with the nearby airbase.

RAF Church Fenton opened on 1st April 1937 while it was still being constructed. It was built as a result of the RAF's massive pre-war expansion in response to Adolf Hitler's move to increase the strength of the German armed forces.

The base was designed as a fighter base from the outset, with the task of protecting the industrial regions of Leeds, Sheffield and Humberside. From the start of the Second World War until August 1940, Church Fenton was a sector station in 13 group, being home to both defensive and offensive squadrons. Due to Church Fenton's remoteness from Southern England it had a limited part in the Battle of Britain, being used as a backup base battle scared fighter squadrons to rest and recuperate.

The airfields main function was to be part of the defensive network of fighter airfields that protected the industrial cities of northern England from attack by German bombers. Throughout the war the airfield was home to any squadrons and aircraft types such as the Spitfire, Hurricane and Mosquito. As with all of the RAF, inevitably a number of Church Fenton aircrew paid the ultimate price in the defence of Britain.

Following the end of the war, the station retained its role as a front line fighter station. In April 1946, the station became one of the first to operate jet aircraft. These were the Gloster Meteors of 263 squadron, and later 257 squadron. In July 1959 the station ceased being a front line home defence station and its role changed to that of pilot training.

The only way to leave the village and return to Leeds is via the train. So with this in mind you need to walk along Station Road and head for the railway station where you can board one of the numerous daily trains back to Leeds to conclude your journey.

The Stags Head Publishing Company (Queensbury) February 2020

The Author can be contacted at montyw111@hotmail.co.uk or

www.facebook.com/markalexanderjacksonhistory/

The Author is also a joint admin of The Facebook group Queensbury

(West Yorkshire) History

Search Amazon for other titles by Mark Alexander Jackson:

Walking Through Bradford's History	2015
County Houses and Murder (Walking Through Wharfedale's History)	2016
The Occasional Leodensian (Walking Through the History of Leeds)	2016
A Raggald and a Russell (Walk Through Queensbury's History)	2017

ISBN: 9798617946354

Printed by Amazon Italia Logistica S.r.l.
Torrazza Piemonte (TO), Italy